Praise for DISCOVER Question

"Questions matter a lot. And, as Deb Calvert's research shows, top sellers use a broader range of questions to create new opportunities and build strong relationships. Honestly, this book makes *SPIN Selling* look like a primer."

- Jill Konrath, author of SNAP Selling and Selling to Big Companies

"This powerful, practical book, based on proven principles for sales success, shows you how to build high levels of trust and credibility from the first moment."

- Brian Tracy, author of Unlimited Sales Success

"Questions are the answer to real success in the field of selling. Planning and practicing the questions you'll ask buyers will make all the difference in the results you get. The real key to success is in asking the questions that will get you the answers you need in determining if and how to serve each client. Discover DISCOVER Questions® and you'll be amazed at how much more fun selling can be."

- Tom Hopkins, author of How to Master the Art of Selling and Selling in Tough Times

"Debra Calvert understands what it took me years to learn; you can have the best questioning model there is, but until you have emotional connection and trust, buyers will not want to answer your questions."

- Mike Bosworth, author of Solution Selling and What Great Salespeople Do

"In sales training, there are many schools of thought. Deb Calvert has created a masterpiece in the school of customer-oriented selling. She puts the spotlight where it belongs—right on the customer. She begins with a section on how to build trust. What better place to start with a customer? She then walks the reader through a journey of discovery of customer needs. The subtlety of her sales logic may escape the casual reader, but not the serious student of sales. Writing a book about questions begins with a simple premise: It must be about the buyer, not the seller. For anyone who wants to learn how to think as their customers think, I recommend reading this book. Your sales life will improve immediately. Congratulations, Deb. You have created a classic."

- Tom Reilly, the guy who wrote the book on Value-Added Selling

"It's one thing to know the right questions and it's quite another to know why to ask them. In *DISCOVER Questions® Get You Connected*, Deb Calvert shows you why and how to become a Question Detective by knowing what to be curious about. And if you are wondering about the right things then the right questions will flow...naturally. Read this book twice and highlight it. Your sales will flow!"

> *- Jim Cathcart, author of the international bestseller Relationship Selling*

"There are hundreds of books about how to build trust, connect with customers, work through your sales process and be more effective in selling. One of the best I've come across is Deb Calvert's *DISCOVER Questions® Get You Connected*. The examples from sales calls, the feedback from buyers, and the fascinating research drive home the importance of asking quality questions. Best of all, the methodology for asking eight types of questions will make every sales conversation you have more natural and more productive. This is a must-read for all sales professionals."

> *- Robert Terson, "retired" sales professional, entrepreneur, sales trainer & coach, author of Selling Fearlessly: A Master Salesman's Secrets For the One-Call-Close Salesperson*

"It was my delight to read Deb Calvert's book, *DISCOVER Questions® Get You Connected*. Deb demonstrates through questioning, a sales representative is able to develop a trustworthy relationship with their potential client. Your added value is the provided knowledge on how to phrase your questions for improved outcomes. These questions dismiss the age old stereotype questions and instead teach how to gain insight on the client's problems and how to help resolve them. In essence, you will read how to best strengthen the relationship and develop trust to enjoy a thriving clientele. This book is a must read for anyone new to sales and provides excellent reminders for those established in their sales career."

> *- Elinor Stutz, Author and Inspirational Keynote Speaker*

"This really is a masterful first book from Deb Calvert: She demonstrates a remarkable understanding of just what it takes to first penetrate the thought process of today's buyer, and to then go on to build a bridge to mutual profitability. The very best sales professionals have an unquenchable thirst for knowledge, which can only be quenched by asking questions, but they ask the right questions at the right time. Those clinging to the outdated information gathering models such as BANT are being left behind, as Debra amply demonstrates. A piece of work that should be digested in its entirety – and then feasted on again and again."

- Jonathan Farrington,
CEO of Top Sales World and Senior Partner of Jonathan Farrington & Associates

"Questions are the sales professional's #1 tool and Deb Calvert's DISCOVER Questions® is the #1 book on sales questions. No book uncovers the science behind the interrogative process better than DISCOVER Questions®. Within these pages is the How and Why of excellent question asking for sales professionals in every industry. You'll learn how to uncover vital information and create value with the questions you ask while establishing trust. If you want to improve your selling effectiveness at the most fundamental level read this book. You won't find a better investment of your time anywhere."

- James Muir, CEO, Best Practice International, Author of The Perfect Close

"If you're looking to drive more sales revenue AND to do it in a way that makes you proud, be sure to read *DISCOVER Questions® Get You Connected*. The sales approach and techniques in this book will help you to genuinely connect with customers by asking strategic, thought-provoking and high-value questions. Deb Calvert shows you how to differentiate yourself by starting with an intent to understand your customer's needs and then she walks you through all the steps you need to make good on your noble intention."

- Lisa Earle McLeod, sales leadership expert and best-selling author of
Selling with Noble Purpose

"One of my favorite sales quotes is..."prescription before diagnosis is malpractice." *DISCOVER Questions® Get You Connected* will help you understand how to diagnose customer needs by using questions to improve your communication, what types of questions to use and when to use them, and the strategies and techniques of artful questioning. Being able to ask the right question at the right time is THE critical piece of the sales process. Questions are the heart of successful sales communication."

- Dr. Tony Alessandra, author of The Platinum Rule for Sales Mastery and
People Smart in Business: Using the DISC Behavioral Styles Model
to Turn Every Business Encounter into a Mutual Win

"During the past few years, a negative trend has developed: less effort is being expended by sellers in *really* understanding their customers as buyers and as people. We all know that selling isn't just telling, but somehow we've strayed from the path. This powerful book serves up a blueprint that gets us back on track—where highly effective and proven discovery skills make the difference between winning and losing. Follow Deb's advice and see your selling behaviors change, resulting in deeper and more mutually beneficial relationships with your customers."

- *Dave Stein*, *CEO and Founder*
ES Research Group, Inc.

"With more demanding and more educated customers than ever before, simple "satisfaction" doesn't build profitable businesses. Loyalty does. Every salesperson that wants to create that true, profitable loyalty with their customers should run out today and get a copy of *DISCOVER Questions® Get You Connected* which is filled with the secrets to finding, attaining and keeping those customers who will stay with you!"

- *Cindy Solomon*, *Customer Loyalty expert, author of The Rules of Woo,*
and creator of the Courageous Leadership programs

"Sales people are always looking for answers, we want information from our customers, we want to know what their problems are, what they think of us, and what it takes to win. But the quality of the answers we get is absolutely dependent on the quality of the questions we ask. Our ability to ask the right questions, in the right way, to the right people at the right time can make the difference between winning and losing. Deb Calvert's book, *DISCOVER Questions® Get You Connected*, is a thoughtful guide to helping sales people get the answers they need and want. Deb takes a deep dive into the different kinds of questions we might ask, what information they elicit, how and when to ask which type of question. The book is a great guide to all sales professionals and should be a desktop reference to anyone who seeks to excel in professional sales."

- *Dave Brock*, *CEO, Partners In EXCELLENCE*

"There's just no doubt about it: If you master questioning and listening skills and authentically connect with your customers, you will serve them better *and* outsell the competition at the same time! Deb Calvert's book gets at the heart of asking the questions that make the greatest difference."

- *Mark Hunter*, *"The Sales Hunter," sales speaker, consultant and author of*
High-Profit Selling: Win the Sale without Compromising on Price

"Too often, salespeople and sales organizations chase the latest and greatest shiny object in search of better sales results. The fundamentals are often abandoned, and we seem to have irrevocably lost some of them for what may have been forever. Enter Deb Calvert and DISCOVER Questions®! When it comes to influencing buying decisions, a good and well placed question is a more powerful tool than any single statement you might make. Read Deb's book. Take time to develop the questions that will allow you to create value for your clients – and win their business!"

> *- Anthony Iannarino, Author, Speaker, Entrepreneur*
> *www.thesalesblog.com*

"Pressured to make quota now, too many sellers try and cut corners in the sales process. Deb Calvert's message is a reminder that success in selling always begins with creating relationships built on trust. You earn that trust by caring about what is important to the buyer and by asking the right questions. In *DISCOVER Questions® Get You Connected*, anyone who sells will benefit from the practical advice shared that is supported with exercises and role plays to help you hone your questioning craft."

> *- Barbara Giamanco, Co-Author of The New Handshake: Sales Meets Social Media*

"There are many books on sales and selling. Deb Calvert, in *DISCOVER Questions® Get You Connected,* has taken the Socratic sales approach to that next level because she has integrated the 21st century demand for connectivity through feeling, thinking and doing. This is a truly simple and yet powerful read."

> *- Leanne Hoagland-Smith, author,*
> *Be the Red Jacket in a Sea of Gray Suits, The Keys to Unlocking Sales Success*

"This is a book that needs not just to be read, but followed. Highly recommend."

> *- Steve Schiffman, Sales Coach, Speaker and Author of over 50 best-selling books*
> *including The Ultimate Book of Sales Techniques*

"Looking back, I was inept at creating deep and meaningful dialogue. Using DISCOVER Questions® has opened so many avenues and healthy discussions for me, both personally and professionally... Being able to use DISCOVER Questions® has also opened the door for me to learn at a faster rate than ever."

> *- Greg Andersen, Produce Sales Manager*

CONNECT MORE TO SELL MORE

Now You Can Be
the One Seller
Buyers WANT to Talk to!

DISCOVER
Questions®
Get You Connected

Volume 1

For Professional Sellers

Deb Calvert

DISCOVER Questions® Get You Connected
Volume 1
For Professional Sellers

Deb Calvert

 Winston Keen James Publishing
Morgan Hill, CA

deb.calvert@peoplefirstps.com
www.peoplefirstps.com

Cover Design and Interior Layout: Renee Calvert

Editorial Consultation: DAAJTHC & Associates

Printed in the United States of America

ISBN: 978-0-9897379-0-6
Library of Congress Number: 2013915057

DISCOVER Questions®
Get You Connected

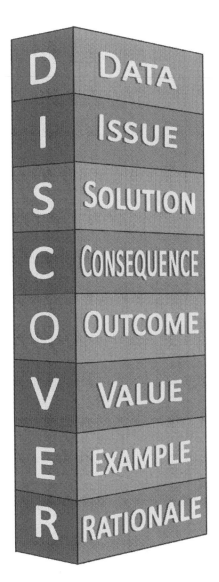

Analysis of over **10,000** sales calls.
25 years of observations and research.
8 types of questions to help you be
the **1** seller buyers WANT to talk to.

DEDICATION

This book is dedicated to my parents, Ronald and Josephine Tibbetts. They always said I'd write a book. But long before I could do that, they determined I would be a salesperson, not professionally but practically.

When I was seven years old, Dad set me up in the cucumber business. We had a huge backyard garden and quite a surplus of cukes that summer. So he loaded up my little red wagon with cucumbers plus a few tomatoes and green peppers. He sent me out to sell our surplus produce door-to-door in the neighborhood. My instructions were: "It's five cents for every item. Don't take any wooden nickels. Come home when everything has been sold, and you can keep the money."

In Missouri, in the heat and humidity of August, going door-to-door pitching vegetables wasn't nearly as much fun as the sales jobs I later held. It was hard work. When a friend rode by on her bicycle, I suggested we sell the produce together and split the proceeds. She was in, and the drudgery was suddenly bearable. We sold everything, and I gave her half the earnings. Then we stopped by a nearby c-store to buy popsicles. When I got home, I got my first official sales training… Dad was not impressed that I had hired another salesperson and split the revenue.

Lesson #1 in selling – you don't split the top line revenue equally with someone who didn't till the soil, plant the seeds, pull the weeds, water every night, fertilize, manage pest control, and pick the product. Even at age seven, I could understand the basic principle of bottom line profit and how a salesperson is responsible for contributing to it.

Mom took over the sales coaching from here. She was my cheerleader, chauffeur, strategist and sales manager during the annual Camp Fire Girl candy-selling season in November-December. Every evening after dinner, we'd set out to canvas neighborhoods, selling Russell Stover candy door-to-door. Buyers had three choices – Peppermint Patties, Assorted Chocolates or Caramel Turtles – for just one dollar a box! Every year for eight straight years, I was the top candy seller in the metro area. It earned me a meeting with the mayor of Kansas City one year and a "campership" for a free week of camping at my beloved Camp Shawnee each summer.

Mom was a good sales coach. She never took over the sale, and she let me flounder and fail as often as necessary. Then she'd offer alternatives about what I might say and how I could be more effective in my sales pitch. I attribute some of her suggestions to her Marine Corps background, including "shoulders back, head up, eyes forward, and speak up!" But I don't know where she learned that asking questions was the most powerful selling technique of all. With her coaching, I'd get people talking. Pretty soon, they were talking themselves into purchasing (many!) boxes of candy.

Our conversations would start like this: "Hello, my name is Debbie. I am selling delicious Russell Stover candies for a limited time so I can raise money for Camp Fire Girls. What are your plans for entertaining and gift-giving during the holiday season?"

Picture this. Here's this little kid on your porch, bundled up against the cold night air, mom standing out on the sidewalk. You're ready to be annoyed at the interruption to your evening when along comes that question. The most common reaction was that an impatient scowl or head shaking "no" would be completely transformed. People would smile, invite me inside, and tell me about their holiday plans. I listened politely, occasionally interjecting information about the candy. (Turtles were my favorite, so I could authentically and strongly recommend them!)

Then they'd start buying. Without hesitation, thanks to Mom's coaching, I would never accept the first number without offering more. But my offer would be in the form of a question. I'd say something like "There are 12 Turtles in each box. How many more boxes will you need to take care of the whole holiday season?"

I've been selling with questions ever since. Mom and Dad are no longer with us, but they are a part of every sale I make and every selling question I ask. That's why this book is dedicated to them.

And, for everything I am and everything I have been able to do, I thank God, my husband, and my children. Their support and encouragement make it possible. My parents set me on this path, and my family has walked this long and winding path with me. This dedication is for their dedication.

CONTENTS

Part I – Connecting Is the Essence of Selling

If you are a successful seller with a depth of experience who consistently uses a needs-based selling approach and asks high-value questions that buyers love, then you may be able to jump straight into Part II of this book. You can always come back to these important fundamentals for a refresher if needed. Just be sure to notice the "IF" that qualifies this conditional permission to read ahead!

Part II – Using DISCOVER Questions ® to Connect

This is the new stuff! Start here if you've already mastered
the fundamentals of needs-based selling!

Part III – Skills Practice

Practice is always optional. But these fun exercises are truly worth your time.

INTRODUCTION

This is a book about selling. It is one of thousands of books written to help selling professionals build essential skills so they can close more sales.

This is also a book about making connections with people, a fundamental skill often overlooked in traditional sales training, books and resource materials. Stereotypes about salespeople cause us to believe that all selling professionals naturally know how to make connections. Training and books start at the next step – what to do **after** a connection has been established.

This assumption handicaps sellers. They may do exactly what they've been trained to do and still fall short. Step-by-step processes fail the seller who does not first establish a solid connection with a buyer.

Complicating matters is the way modern buyers demand more from sellers. Today, buyers are empowered because they have more options, more access, ease of comparison shopping, and instant reviews at their fingertips. In a tight economy, sellers have to work harder to demonstrate competitive differentiation and to add genuine value for demanding buyers.

One of the demands buyers are making more frequently is they want to work with sellers they can connect with and trust. This means buyers want sellers who are knowledgeable about their own products **and** knowledgeable about the buyer's needs and situation, too.

It's a tall order. To be successful, sellers absolutely must make a different kind of connection with their buyers.

Genuinely connecting with buyers goes beyond superficial selling relationships. A seller may know his customer enjoys baseball, and they may enjoy a casual exchange about the home team before they move into the sales conversation. But this is no longer a sufficient connection to advance the sale to a close.

Connecting with buyers also goes beyond describing features and benefits. A seller may know a buyer routinely needs a particular product, and the seller may do a fine job of articulating how the features of her product will deliver certain benefits to the buyer. But this too is insufficient for making a connection to advance the sale to a close.

A meaningful connection between the buyer and the seller, as described by buyers, will include:

- Sellers are respectful of their buyers' time.

- Sellers customize their presentations, making them highly relevant for each buyer.

- Sellers add value by making every engagement more than a sales transaction.

- Sellers listen and understand what their buyers need.

- Sellers ask questions that make buyers think in new ways.

- Sellers collaborate with their buyers to create innovative solutions.

- Sellers probe to understand more about business needs so they can continually offer more relevance, more value and more collaboration.

This is a far cry from the age-old standards of pitch selling. It is no longer effective for sellers to make generic presentations, to overcome a few objections and then to push for a close. Buyers aren't responding to this approach, and they never will again.

This book will help sellers fill in the gaps and make the connections they need with buyers. In order to truly connect with buyers, sellers need to know how to ask strategic questions that are respectful, time-efficient, relevant, stimulating, value-adding and collaborative. The questions sellers ask must stand alone to create value by making buyers think. DISCOVER Questions® are the key to making these kinds of connections.

DISCOVER Questions® were developed over 25 years of analyzing questions and how they are used in selling. As a seller, sales manager, sales trainer, sales field coach, and sales organization consultant, author Deb Calvert has captured the questions asked during 10,000+ sales calls. She analyzed each question and what it yielded in terms of buyer response. She interviewed buyers and got their feedback about the questions asked. Then she grouped questions and identified eight discrete types of questions sellers can use strategically to improve their connections with buyers.

DISCOVER Questions® will transform the way you sell and the way you are perceived by buyers. This approach has been field tested with thousands of professional sellers. Like them, you will become more proficient in the way you craft your questions. You will diversify the types of questions you ask so you get more information more quickly as you facilitate thought-provoking discussions with buyers. As your conversations improve, your connections will strengthen. You will be the one seller buyers WANT to talk to.

PART I
CONNECTING IS THE ESSENCE OF SELLING

If you are a successful seller with a depth of experience who consistently uses a needs-based selling approach and asks high-value questions that buyers love, then you may be able to jump straight into Part II of this book. You can always come back to these important fundamentals for a refresher if needed. The chapters in Parts II and III tell you where to turn back for specific refreshers.

On the other hand, why not skim through this section? Other highly experienced and outrageously successful sellers have discovered valuable nuggets here that could help you, too.

| Responses from real buyers | Scripts from actual sales calls | Examples of questions |

CHAPTER 1
Connect by Building Trust

You cannot form solid connections without a firm foundation of trust. Trust brings buyers and sellers together and keeps them together. A lack of trust inhibits buyers, and a breach in trust shuts them down completely. Trust is vital to forming buyer/seller connections.

When it comes to establishing trust, sellers start with a disadvantage. It isn't fair, but it's an unavoidable reality. The profession of selling has a blemished reputation. Buyers have been conditioned to proceed with caution when entering into relationships with sellers. Buyers assume sellers are money-motivated, tricky, slick and self-absorbed. All too often, sellers prove these perceptions to be true. So the rest of us have to compensate for untrustworthy ones who burn our buyers.

In order to gain and maintain the trust of buyers, sellers must act in a trustworthy manner at all times. Trust is so fragile that a 90% rate of being trustworthy simply isn't good enough. The buyer will remember the one out of 10 times you did not deliver in a trustworthy way.

The 12 Dimensions of Trust

100% trustworthy is a mighty high standard. On top of that, there's more to being trustworthy than you might expect. There are 12 different dimensions of trust that come into play. Knowing and being responsive in all 12 areas is what it takes to build and preserve trust. DISCOVER Questions® can help you do exactly that.

These 12 Dimensions of Trust are explained in Illustration #1 on page 4. The descriptions following the table include how you can use questions to build trust in 12 ways. As you review the Dimensions of Trust, you may be surprised by what's included. Most of us start and end with a narrower definition focused on honesty and integrity. But understanding how trustworthiness is also evaluated on follow through, availability, self-assessment and more can help sellers improve the way they are perceived and received by their buyers.

The 12 Dimensions of Trust

Competence	Seller's skills & knowledge are commensurate with expected results. Seller strives to learn and increase competence.
Integrity	Seller consistently makes ethical choices regardless of convenience, profit, fun or other personal benefit.
Consistency	Seller is reliable, steady, predictable. Everyone knows what to expect from this person. Seller is someone you can count on.
Loyalty	Seller makes and keeps long-term commitments to individuals, teams and organizations; supports others at all times.
Availability	Seller makes time for needed conversations and listens without distractions. Seller is fully present in interactions.
Fairness	Seller uses objective criteria to evaluate situation or people. Does not exhibit favoritism, holds everyone to equal standards.
Decision-Making	Seller knows & shares decision-making criteria. Involves others in decision-making process. Explains rationale of decisions.
Follow Through	Seller delivers what has been promised. Honors agreements. Accepts responsibility if commitments are not kept.
Openness	Seller communicates with complete disclosure, doesn't hold back information. Shares opinion even when it's not popular.
Discretion	Seller respects confidentiality. Seller gets permission, uses care before sharing information with others.
Constructive Intent	Seller shares sensitive messages without causing defensiveness. Seller's communication motives are not self-serving.
Accurate Self-Assessment	Seller understands and acknowledges his or her own limitations, seeks and accepts help when needed.

Illustration 1

These 12 Dimensions of Trust represent the 12 ways a seller can build or erode trust with buyers. Each associated action creates a connection or causes a disconnection. Knowing about all 12 Dimensions of Trust empowers a seller who wants strong connections founded in trust. Not knowing leads to buyer mistrust and seller confusion.

Confused sellers disconnect by responding ineffectively when buyers express a lack of trust. Buyers' suspicions or reservations may not seem warranted. The seller may not be able to pinpoint what action(s) led to diminished trust. The seller may also be reluctant to acknowledge how his or her own action(s) were a factor in diminishing the buyer's trust. Not understanding the 12 Dimensions of Trust can convolute the situation and result in misplaced blame instead of corrective action.

One common example is when a buyer says "This didn't work like you told me it would." The implied loss of trust could be related to the product's failure or to the seller's failure in setting reasonable expectations. Buyers start with the belief that sellers have exaggerated or made false claims about their products. Sellers who don't know all 12 Dimensions of Trust don't hold themselves accountable in this situation. Instead, they believe their products are unsatisfactory.

The problem with this scenario is two-fold. First, the buyer's trust is broken, the relationship is impaired, and the blame is reported internally as a dissatisfaction with the product. That means subsequent sales attempts are less likely. Second, the seller is not likely to self-correct, so this scenario will be recurring. With enough repetition, the seller will truly believe the product is flawed or inferior.

To avoid misplacing blame and to build trust, sellers need to become more self-aware and cognizant of the 12 Dimensions of Trust.

As you read more about each of the 12 Dimensions of Trust, note how several could be subjectively interpreted in different ways by different people.

This is why it's so important to ask quality questions to clarify and build trust. A seller who asks questions to understand how a buyer perceives a situation can help minimize any misunderstanding. Doing so prevents a breach of trust. Similarly, trust can be improved in every dimension when sellers ask questions about buyer expectations, preferences and needs.

Sellers can put questions to work with each dimension in these ways:

1. Competence

"Seller strives to learn and increase competence" is best demonstrated by asking questions. Being interested and curious naturally leads to asking questions. Buyers do not mind educating sellers, so long as the learning is proactive and improves a seller's ability to serve the buyer.

Sellers sometimes avoid asking questions because they don't want to seem uninformed. They opt, instead, to act on limited information. In the long run, this strategy usually backfires and can make a seller seem incompetent. You are always more effective when you ask questions to learn more about your buyer.

Questions demonstrate competence. Use what you know to build your knowledge and showcase your level of expertise. A seller who says "Tell me more about the sustainability initiatives you're planning" will seem far more competent than the one who neglects to ask.

2. Integrity

"Seller consistently makes ethical choices" seems straightforward. But two different people looking at the same situation from two different perspectives might interpret this differently. For example, a seller once sacrificed his entire weekend to undo an error so his customer's order would be perfectly executed. He literally worked day and night to get everything in place, and he fulfilled on over 99% of the order.

Unfortunately, as luck would have it, one of the few remaining products with an error shipped to the buyer's own home address. When the buyer learned about the seller's sacrifice in trying to deliver, the buyer perceived the seller's actions as deceitful rather than as high integrity. Why? Because the seller did not tell the buyer what was going on ahead of time. He worked hard to avoid the embarrassment of admitting a mistake. He thought he acted with integrity by trying to make it right. The buyer felt differently.

Questions asked ahead of time would have helped the seller understand the buyer's perspective. Here's a question few sellers ask in their initial needs assessment: "In the unlikely event of an error, how and when would you like to be notified?" One seller who asked this question for the first time was pleasantly surprised when the buyer smiled and said "No one has ever asked me that before! Thank you for checking ahead of time just in case you need to know."

3. Consistency

"Seller is reliable, steady, predictable" sounds positive, but it could also be limiting at a time when buyers are demanding new ideas from sellers. To differentiate yourself from other reliable, steady, predictable sellers who show up and pitch products the same way every time, use quality questions to stimulate discussion and to make buyers think in new ways.

Consider asking your buyers what's working and should remain the same in the way you handle the account. Ask, too, what's not working and needs to change. Be reliable, steady and predictable in your desire to routinely meet your buyers' needs.

4. Loyalty

"Seller supports others at all times" includes providing what others want and need. As a seller, one powerful way to support buyers is by asking them questions to challenge their assumptions and help them discover alternate ways of addressing their problems.

7

A transactional order-taker who does not form relationships with buyers is done once the order is placed. But a seller who connects with buyers long term must show genuine interest and support to demonstrate and engender loyalty.

I recently switched hair salons for this very reason. My former stylist supported me by getting me in on short notice, and I enjoyed our conversations about our children and our travels. But I didn't feel she could "get me to the next level."

By contrast, my new stylist supported me right from the start. In our initial conversations, she challenged me when I said "I need to spend five minutes or less on styling my hair each morning." Her challenge was direct, and it made me think. She asked "How's that been working for you so far?" and "What's more important – the amount of time or the image you present?"

> Asking questions and listening actively to the responses is an investment of time, not a waste of time.

By taking time to help me work out my own competing priorities, she supported me in a way my former stylist did not.

Supporting your buyers means you help them through their difficulties and challenges. To support means "to supply with things necessary" and "to provide for." Your buyers don't exist to support you. They do business with sellers who can, in some way, support them. DISCOVER Questions® give you a tool to support your buyers.

5. Availability

"Seller makes time for needed conversations and listens without distractions" is a particularly difficult assignment for sellers. In an informal poll of sales trainers and sales managers, the question "why don't more sellers ask more questions more often?" was answered over and over again with the responses "sellers don't have time" and "buyers don't have time." But by not asking

8

questions, sellers waste considerably more of their own time and the time of buyers as they present off-the-mark solutions and then regroup to make modified proposals and to overcome objections they should have anticipated and avoided.

Asking questions and listening actively to the responses is an investment of time, not a waste of time.

A seller who makes the time to conduct a thorough needs assessment and routinely checks in by asking follow-up questions builds trust and conveys availability and interest in the buyers' needs. This doesn't have to be laborious or time consuming. Just a few quality questions can turn every sales call into a trust-building connection.

6. Fairness

"Seller does not exhibit favoritism" means a seller will not make assumptions about one buyer based on the information gathered from another buyer. Giving each individual buyer an opportunity to describe his or her own wants, needs and interests builds trust by making him or her feel special. Additionally, this unique information enables the seller to provide more relevant solutions to each and every buyer.

To uncover the unique needs, wants and interests of each individual buyer necessitates asking quality questions yielding actionable information. Instead of clustering her buyers by age, income and marital status like her predecessor had, one sales agent for a retirement living community decided to "start from scratch" with each prospect. Even though the demographic profile was an accurate predictor for placement, this agent's close rate was significantly higher. Why?

Because buyers felt, as one said, "We were treated here like people, not like old people being herded all together but like individual people who are unique and special."

9

7. Decision-Making

"Seller involves others in decision-making process" happens when a seller is transparent and shares with the buyer what steps will be happening behind the scenes. One seller paid attention when an apprehensive buyer applied for a line of credit. The seller asked questions to understand the buyer's reservations. This led to a thorough explanation of the screening process and the seller facilitating a call between the buyer and the credit manager. When the credit application was denied, the buyer understood why and expressed appreciation for the openness the seller exhibited. The buyer contrasted this to other sellers who divorced themselves from the process and refused to get involved, making it seem they didn't really care.

8. Follow Through

"Seller honors agreements" is another potentially gray and subjective area. It is impossible to honor an agreement unless it is clearly and mutually understood by both parties. Asking questions to confirm who will do what can help ensure good follow through.

> Buyers expect sellers to support them by bringing new ways of looking at old problems.

Outlining action items, along with deliverable dates, is a good sales practice and should be followed by questions like "What have I missed?" and "What else would you like for me to do?"

9. Openness

"Seller shares opinion even when it's not popular" has become a must-do practice of selling. Buyers expect sellers to support them by bringing new ways of looking at old problems. They also expect sellers to be candid and to fully disclose their own opinions. Because time is precious, buyers don't want to do business with sellers who have nothing new to say.

One way to offer new information effectively is to ask strategic questions prompting buyers to do their own thinking and discovering. This is particularly important for sellers who don't have entirely new ideas and for those who aren't sure how a buyer will react to a new idea. Questions can plant seeds, test the waters and open up the dialogue, making it easier for a seller to share opinions – even those which may not be well-received.

Asking "what alternatives have you considered?" and "what are your thoughts about ____?" create opportunities for opening up conversations. Before you share your opinion, you'll have insights into the buyer's likely reaction. This proactive step ensures empathy and effectiveness as you share your opinion.

10. Discretion

"Seller gets permission, uses care before sharing information with others" is a frequently missed dimension of trust. In an effort to close the deal, a seller sometimes divulges to a prospect what competitors are buying. This may be effective in getting a buyer's attention and even in compelling a close. But it also leaves a residual feeling of mistrust. If the seller is sharing the competitor's information, the buyer realizes his or her information might be shared, too.

Trust is built when questions are used to erect walls around what is confidential. Asking "Would you mind if I shared this?" is professional and courteous. Asking "How much can I share about you with your competitor?" is a fair response when a buyer asks a seller to share confidential information about someone else.

11. Constructive Intent

"Seller shares sensitive messages without causing defensiveness" is also commonly overlooked as sellers attempt to build trust with buyers. Without meaning to, sellers come across as insensitive because they haven't learned what triggers defensiveness or emotional responses in their buyers. This can happen when questions are poorly sequenced, ill-conceived or badly crafted. Before we introduce DISCOVER Questions®, we'll look at how to craft questions so your constructive intent is conveyed.

Questions asked to uncover past issues between the buyer and seller companies, pet peeves the buyer may have and preferred service protocols help a seller to be proactive and avoid causing unproductive buyer reactions.

12. Accurate Self-Assessment

"Seller seeks and accepts help when needed" goes hand-in-hand with "strives to learn" and the first dimension of trust, competence. A seller must be competent and also willing to acknowledge his or her own deficits. Over-estimating one's own abilities results in sub-par performance, delays and missed opportunities. Asking questions to understand what is expected and what alternatives are acceptable will help sellers see more clearly what resources they will need in order to fully satisfy their buyers.

Trust will be cemented by asking quality questions. This is true in selling relationships just as it is in personal relationships. Think about someone you trust. Consider the way he or she interacts with you. Chances are good the person you trust asks you thought-provoking questions and challenges your status quo. Chances are good, too, that you trust this individual more – and certainly not less – as a direct result of those questions.

We trust people who ask quality questions because questions convey personal interest. We are more willing to trust people who have taken time to be personally interested in us. Questions communicate our interest. Questions position us to deliver on all 12 Dimensions of Trust.

When a buyer trusts you, the idea of doing business with someone else loses its appeal. Trust is like super glue for buyer/seller relationships. Trust forms unbreakable bonds, and that's the kind of connection you want with every buyer.

CHAPTER 2
They Don't Care How Much You Know
Until They Know How Much You Care

Before the advent of the Internet, buyers relied heavily on sellers to provide product specifications and information. Sellers were the experts and were often the sole source for placing product orders.

With the Internet, the role of the seller has been diminished. Buyers now rely on their peers – other buyers – to provide first-hand knowledge and user experiences. Buyers can order online and completely avoid dealing with sellers. Buyers can also research and compare features, prices, add-ons and options before placing an order with a seller.

Sellers have been slow to catch up to this new reality.

Despite the fact that buyers are educating themselves, sellers still open sales calls by assuming buyers need to be educated. Buyers see this as a waste of time, and it fuels their aversion to meeting with sellers.

Despite the fact that buyers can easily complete transactional purchases online, sellers are not taking steps to add value to the sales process. By missing the opportunity to add value, a seller fails to enhance or express competitive differentiation. This commoditizes the product, regardless of how superior it may be.

Sellers bear a greater responsibility than ever before when it comes to marketing their products. Since buyers are not as brand loyal as they used to be (aside from a few exceptions like Apple), they are more focused on price and more fickle when something new or different comes along. A seller who doesn't differentiate a product by expressing its key benefits – the benefits that are uniquely relevant to each individual buyer – inadvertently reinforces the notion that one brand is no different from another.

13

Sellers do their companies, products and buyers a disservice if they perpetuate these insidious notions.

Worse yet, sellers do a disservice to all selling professionals when they don't purposefully differentiate themselves by adding value to each and every sales encounter. Unfortunately, the plethora of sales enablement and artificial intelligence tools and social media options depersonalize selling when sellers fail to truly connect with buyers and positively differentiate themselves. Why? In part because buyers will no longer see the need to interact with sellers.

Given the way buyers feel about sellers, building trust and bringing value to every interaction is not optional for sellers. Using DISCOVER Questions® and the connection skills in Part I of this book will ensure you are one seller buyers want to spend time with.

Adding Value

Adding value to a sales call – even a brief telephone call – is not difficult. It doesn't cost a penny. It does require a deliberate focus on caring about what would be of interest to this particular buyer at this moment in time. Adding value means first understanding what would be valued.

This term "added value" means different things to different people. Some describe added value as bundling in additional features or options, often at no extra charge. Others describe added value as a giveaway or deal sweetener like box seats at a ball game or promotions to reward top clients with incentives. Still others describe value added as a preferred status or higher level partnership given to a few select customers.

> For some buyers this "value added" was actually "value subtracted."

The basic meaning of adding value is simpler. Adding value is something every seller can (and should!) do in every selling encounter. To add value means to bring a little extra to the meeting – not extra product or extra incentives necessarily, but extra **value**. To know what will be valued by your buyer, you'd first have to find out what your buyer values. Don't make generalities or assumptions. Make it personal when it comes to value.

Value is unique to every single buyer. Sellers tend to make assumptions and over-rely on generic value instead of discovering what is uniquely valued by each individual buyer. That's why they miss the mark.

Consider the professional directory listings sales rep who started each call by saying "I have a value-added offer for you. If you sign up today, I can offer you a bold-type header for your listing."

INSIDE THE SALES CALL

It's not a bad offer as the price to buy bold type ranged from $750 to $2500 (depending on the total distribution of the selected directory). But the value didn't resonate with all buyers because different people value different things. For some buyers this "value added" was actually "value subtracted."

Some buyers value time more than they value savings. Being pressed to make this decision on a day when they are already overwhelmed with deadlines and deliverables on other projects is value-subtracting, not value-adding, for these buyers. On another day, when these buyers do get around to making the purchase, they feel they have lost something. It bothers them to proceed with the purchase knowing there is less to it.

Some buyers value image more than they value savings. They don't want their listing to be presented looking the same as so many others. Learning that bold type is widely available at no extra cost makes it unappealing to these buyers. This subtracts value rather than adding value because it increases the effort required to stand out more than all these bold type listings will.

Some buyers value creativity more than they value savings. Learning that the single line of bold type is only available in the header when they would

15

prefer to have it in their tag line makes it value-subtracting. The inflexibility of the so-called "value-added offer" is unsatisfying to this creative type.

The list goes on. When something generic is offered to everyone, not everyone will appreciate the value equally.

Questions Reveal What's Valued

Using questions to understand what buyers value is smart strategy for sellers. By asking just one or two questions to understand what an individual values and the hierarchy or priority of what is valued, a seller demonstrates he or she cares about the unique buyer.

The old maxim applies here. **They don't care how much you know until they know how much you care.**

This is why the top performer is not necessarily the one who knows the product line best. Superior product knowledge can even be a trap, leading to an over-dependence on reciting facts and figures about the product's bells and whistles. In organizations that provide lots of product training without also offering solid sales training, it is not uncommon for sales managers to be perplexed about why sellers aren't hitting their numbers.

The answer is in that maxim. Sellers who pitch products are only showing what they know. And buyers don't care.

What makes a buyer care is knowing the seller cares. This can't be generic, it can't be faked, and it can't be robotically built in to a sales pitch. It doesn't come from a one-time process that is scripted or routinized. It has to come from actually caring about the individual buyer.

Caring about the buyer means the seller wants to understand enough to offer solutions that will solve the buyer's most urgent and pressing needs.

Caring about the buyer means the seller wants to go "above and beyond" to differentiate himself or herself and earn the buyer's business. Caring about the buyer means the seller is looking for repeat business, referrals and satisfied customers rather than taking a "win at all costs" approach.

There is no better way to show how much you care than by understanding and responding to a buyer's unique needs and what he or she personally values. There is only one way

> **Questions equip sellers to truly add value.**

to find out about an individual's needs and value priorities. That's by asking questions. Questions equip sellers to truly add value.

This is significantly different from pitching generic features and trying to extend them into generic benefits. Contrast the presentations of a product feature to see how much difference a focus on personalized value can make.

Seller A

"This model has electronic stability control that helps the driver maintain control in an extreme steering maneuver. ESC will automatically brake on one wheel when you get into an over-steering or plow out situation."

Seller B

INSIDE THE SALES CALL

"Because you have a safety concern about your teenaged drivers, I'd like to tell you about the electronic stability control that's available on this model. ESC will be an added protection if one of your new drivers gets into a situation where they need to course correct but over-correct by turning the steering wheel too sharply. It will give you peace of mind when your new drivers are out on their own."

Both Seller A and Seller B believed they were presenting a feature and a benefit. Seller A did, in fact, present the feature exactly as he was trained to do, and he gave more information about the electronic stability control than Seller B did. Seller A thought "automatically braking" was the benefit.

Actually, though, this is just a feature of the feature. It may imply a benefit, but it requires the buyer to connect the dots in order to figure out the relevant benefit and its associated value.

Seller B did not assume the implied benefit would be clear. He asked questions at the beginning of the meeting to ascertain who would be driving the car and what mattered most to the buyer. Armed with specific information, he presented the feature in a different way than Seller A did. Seller B knew the benefit that would matter to this particular buyer at this particular time, and he spelled it out by explaining how "it will give you peace of mind."

> **Any time a seller can ask a few strategic questions that reveal a buyer's needs and primary values, the seller can personalize value.**

Seller B presented this same feature to another buyer later the same day in an entirely different way. Same feature, different benefit, to highlight the value for a different buyer. Here's what Seller B said in the second presentation:

Seller B (to a different buyer)

"Let me show you something that will alleviate your fears about winter driving here. Since you're not accustomed to driving in the snow and ice, this will be a backup system for you until you've got a few Minnesota winters under your belt. What this does is correct the steering and braking when the car goes into a skid. Research is saying that 95% of fatal accidents that started with a skid could have been prevented with this technology."

INSIDE THE SALES CALL

Same feature. Same day. Different buyer. Different benefits. Anytime a seller can ask a few strategic questions that reveal a buyer's needs and primary values, the seller can personalize value.

Both presentations by Seller B caused the buyers to say they felt as if they'd been heard and understood. They felt their needs were being taken seriously and would be met. They trusted Seller B.

Seller A's buyer didn't feel the same way. Instead, she was bored and felt overwhelmed by the uninteresting and irrelevant data. She said it seemed like he was saying what someone told him to say without any regard to what she wanted.

You can probably guess who made several sales that day and who did not.

Buyers don't care how much you know until they know how much you care. To show how much you care, you need to ask quality questions, listen carefully to the answers, and then make links between your solution or product offering and the buyer's unique needs.

This starts with an investment of time on the front end of the sales process. But it saves considerable time later in the sales process. You will ask questions instead of struggling with ceaseless objections. You will personalize value instead of reciting a litany of irrelevant features. Over time, you will develop trust, leading to referrals and returning customers instead of cold calling for every sale.

Ultimately, you will be selling the way modern buyers demand. You will be adding value every time you meet with a buyer. By doing so, you will also be differentiating yourself and positively representing your company.

CHAPTER 3
Aligning Your Sales Process with the Buyer's Process

You may be surprised to learn the buyer has a process, too. You're probably familiar with this progression whether or not you've called it the buyer's process in the past.

In order to connect with buyers, sellers need to align with them. Once a connection gets out of alignment, sales fall apart. This misalignment is at the root of many lost sales. It happens when:

- Sellers hear an expression of mild interest and race ahead to try and close the sale.

- Sellers feel time is limited and present features in a rapid-fire method some call "show up and throw up."

- Sellers presume everyone is familiar with their products and brands.

- Sellers miss buying signals and continue to sell after the buyer is ready to take action (sometimes un-selling a sold buyer!).

- Sellers mistakenly view objections or questions as a lack of interest rather than as an expression of interest.

Paying attention to where a buyer is in the buying process is also a way to show you care. Focusing on the buyer and tracking the stage of the process he or she is in helps the seller to maintain alignment. This prevents the feeling a buyer may have of being rushed or of not being heard and understood.

DISCOVER Questions® can steer a buyer through their own buying process. Questions are also useful for a seller who wants to check where the buyer is. By asking questions to track the buyer's current position, a seller maintains alignment. This may seem like you are creating more work but taking this extra step actually reduces your selling time. You'll be decreasing confusion and increasing the likelihood of a closed sale with a satisfied buyer.

The Buyer's Process

The Buyer's Process includes just four steps. They are:

Awareness

In order to buy something, the buyer must first be aware it exists. Awareness can start with the product itself or with the company's brand.

Interest

Once buyers develop awareness, they may or may not progress in their buying process to develop an interest in the product.

Desire

Once interested, a buyer may come to desire the product. Wanting the product will cause the buyer to consider options for acquiring it.

Action

With sufficient desire, the buyer will take the actions required to purchase the product.

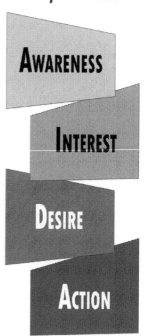

The Buyer's Process

AWARENESS

INTEREST

DESIRE

ACTION

Illustration 2

The buyer's process is simple. It can all happen within milliseconds. It may take longer to explain the process of this chewing gum purchase than it would actually take for the process to occur. Imagine a buyer standing in the checkout line at a grocery store. While in line, the buyer becomes aware that a new flavor of chewing gum has been stocked in the checkout line. It carries a familiar brand name. The buyer is interested by the unique flavor which triggers a desire to taste the gum. The buyer reaches out and takes the action of putting a package of this gum into her shopping cart.

With bigger ticket purchases – those that can take months to complete – the buyer's process is also evident. When purchasing a new home, for example, a buyer first becomes aware one is for sale. After gathering information about the schools, neighborhood and selling price, the buyer may be interested enough to proceed. After touring the home with a real estate agent, the buyer's interest may be growing into desire. If that desire is sufficient, the buyer will take the action of making an offer on the property.

Aligning with the Buyer's Process

In order to be aligned with the buyer's process, the seller must first understand it and then continually gauge where the buyer is. In doing so, a seller will:

- Check the buyer's **awareness** level before jumping into a sales presentation so as not to bore the buyer with information that is already known nor to skip over critical information the buyer will need to develop interest.

- Gather information about the buyer in order to present relevant product details that will stimulate **interest.**

- Create and magnify **desire** by focusing on the product features which are of the highest interest to the buyer, linking them to needs and values and priorities for this unique buyer at this moment in time.

- Notice buying signals that are expressions of desire signaling an intent to take **action** and move in tandem with the buyer toward a close.

Sellers who are caught up in their own sales process frequently fail to stay aligned in these fundamental ways. Asking questions will slow the seller down just enough to monitor where the buyer is in his or her own process.

More often than not, misalignment occurs when sellers focus on the buyer's final step, action. Training that emphasizes techniques like "ABC – Always Be Closing" forces a seller to get ahead of the buyer. When a buyer feels pressured

> **Sellers who are caught up in their own sales process frequently fail to stay aligned in these fundamental ways.**

due to premature closing attempts, the buyer's interest will wane. Left with only awareness and annoyance, the buyer may abandon the purchase altogether.

In their eagerness to close sales, sellers may also misinterpret mild or casual interest for desire. The buyer who is interested will ask non-committal questions or may make vague statements about the product. By contrast, a buyer who has developed desire for a product will ask much more specific questions and will make statements that are quite detailed about how he or she would use a product.

Notice the differences in the kinds of questions and statements offered here as examples to contrast what an interested buyer would say vs. what a buyer with desire would say. The seller who recognizes these subtle differences in live time during a sales call will stay aligned with the buyer.

What an interested buyer would say:

- How long has this been on the market?

- I wonder who uses this sort of thing.

- I remember hearing something about that from my boss.

- Oh! Isn't that cute?

- How does this work exactly?

What a buyer with desire would say:

- Do you offer any sort of financing?

- What additional colors are available?

- How long does it take to configure and install?

- I think that would be a perfect fit in my dining room.

- That would help us reduce downtime.

Listening closely to word choice and asking questions to confirm will prevent a seller from rushing a buyer. The seller who is aligned gives the buyer a feeling of being understood and respected.

To advance the sale smoothly, a seller must track the buyer's progression through the buyer's process. Misalignment results in severed connections, breaches of trust and lost sales. Never let your sales process override your buyer's process.

CHAPTER 4
Value Is Inherently Personal

No two people value the same thing, in the same proportion, at the same time, for the same reasons. Value is inherently personal. Our perceptions about what we value are rooted in our personal histories and influenced by our present circumstances.

In addition to being inherently personal, value is also transitory. What we value changes with every life event and as a result of others' value judgments, too. What we value is not the same as what our values are. Values – the ideals we hold

> **In addition to being inherently personal, value is also transitory.**

like honesty or family-focus – may never change. What we value refers to the desired outcome or result of our work and efforts.

Our values may, of course, influence what we value. Someone with a faith-based ideal might strive to achieve a highly-valued outcome of being able to support missionary work, for example. But that desired outcome could change if a pressing need were to arise for support within the local church or if the same person experienced a significant life change like becoming a parent. But that's not to say all new parents automatically experience a shift in value. Because value is personal, we can't make generalizations or assumptions.

All this is also true of buyers. What they value is influenced by their own personal experiences and ideals. The outcomes they desire are transitory, dependent on job pressures, life circumstances, other projects, input from other team members, and current company priorities. It is a mistake to assume what was valued at one time is still valued with equal importance the next time. Since value is what spurs a buyer to move from interest to desire to action, a smart seller will check on value frequently and keep current with the buyer's current priorities.

What Does Your Buyer Value Today?

Asking questions reveals what a buyer values and to what degree. Questions about value should be routinely asked to confirm that what was important is still important. A proactive seller who identifies a new value early on has the advantage of being the first seller with a chance to meet the needs driven by this new value paradigm. On the other hand, a seller who misses a change may be left out in the cold when the buyer moves on to work with another seller who identified the value and created a solution supporting the new value.

To illustrate how this can happen, put yourself in the shoes of a sales rep who worked with the same account for nearly 15 years. The seller believed she knew the account better than anyone. She visited frequently and had established an ease and comfort level with the buyer. She sheltered the account from sales blitzes and "mandatory" add-ons, defended the account against price increases and promotions, and maintained the status quo in every possible way.

INSIDE THE SALES CALL

This seller genuinely felt she was meeting the needs of her long-term customer. But by shielding the customer from new information and continuing to operate on old assumptions, the seller lost the account. She was blindsided when she stopped by one Tuesday afternoon, just as she had on every Tuesday afternoon for many years. The buyer was apologetic and tried to let her down easily by saying "We needed some fresh ideas and a new way of doing things. We're switching to your competitor because they offer expedited delivery and different packaging sizes."

Stunned, the seller could only say "We offer those things, too, but I know saving money is important to you so I never bothered you with those pitches."

The buyer's response was delivered in a disappointed and scolding tone. He said "You know we've always liked doing business with you. But who are you to make decisions like that for us?"

What was valued had changed for the buyer. The seller had become complacent and hadn't checked in to understand emerging needs or to understand how what was valued had changed in the face of new competitive pressures. Her intentions may have been good, but her actions hurt her customer's business and cost her company (and her personally) a major account that should have been a lifetime customer.

Sellers who keep abreast of value changes make it clear, over and over again, that they respect and are attuned to what their buyers care about most. This creates trust and connection. It also differentiates the seller and reveals new opportunities for additional sales. If a seller does not know what a buyer values, the seller is destined to make costly errors. Understanding what your buyer values is not optional.

At a minimum, at all times, a seller should know the following:

- What the buyer's top priority is within their buying role.

- What the buyer is motivated by in his or her personal life.

- What the buyer values about the seller's product.

- What the buyer values about the seller and the seller's company.

- What recent changes may influence what is valued.

To anticipate what a prospect or new buyer might value, a seller should be mindful of these factors:

- What is the buyer's job title and what do people with this job title usually focus on most?

29

- What is the buyer responsible for delivering and to whom?

- How will the buyer's performance be measured?

- What is the buyer's history with the seller's company?

- What is personally important to the buyer?

A seller should not, however, make assumptions based on these factors. These are starting points so a seller can begin probing with a clear focus. Any assumptions made based on these factors could backfire and land the seller in the same position as the seller in our previous example.

In practice, the seller would have some preliminary ideas based on these factors and would ask strategic questions designed to check assumptions and provide a greater depth of understanding. Here's how it looks, step-by-step.

Step 1: Seller reviews available information

A seller is going to be calling on the regional manager for a furniture chain. The seller knows regional managers are charged with driving year-over-year same-store sales increases. The seller also knows it is common practice in this company to promote only regional managers who consistently perform. Those who do not deliver increases are demoted to store manager positions or to smaller regions. The seller also knows this

INSIDE THE SALES CALL

regional manager used to work for another chain. In between working for the two furniture chains, the seller recalls the buyer took a leave of absence after having twins.

Step 2: Seller resists the urge to pitch prematurely

This is a good amount of information. Many sellers would create a pitch based on this knowledge alone, emphasizing the need to deliver on sales goals and referencing how reaching goals would mean more money to put into the college fund for the twins. Even if all this were accurate, it would still be a diluted sales approach – watered down because it was the seller, not the buyer, who declared what was important.

Step 3: Seller checks information and assumptions

A better approach would be to ask questions to confirm the assumptions and get the buyer talking. Questions like "Tell me about the goals you're faced with and how you're performing year-to-date" will yield new information and heighten the buyer's interest. Questions like "What will it mean to you and your family if you achieve these goals?" also yield keen insights with the additional advantage of showing the buyer the seller understands and is interested in learning more.

> The answers given by the buyer make a much stronger sales presentation than the seller's words.

Step 4: Seller uses buyer's responses to create a solid solution

The answers given by the buyer make a much stronger sales presentation than the seller's words ever could. We are all more committed to what we ourselves have thought and expressed. When the buyer hears her own reasons and sees how the seller can link what she values to what he has to offer, it will be hard for her to say "no" to such a compelling sales case. Consider what caused you to read this book. The author, who may have a personal agenda to sell books, is less credible than the sales professionals who endorsed the book and are quoted. Even they were less convincing than someone you know who personally recommended the book. But YOU are the person you believed. You had your own reason for reading this book, and that's why you are.

The seller who understands value and taps into it like this is adept in moving the buyer through the buying process, from interest to desire and from desire to action. By putting what the buyer values at the heart of the sale, the seller steadily advances the sale to a close.

CHAPTER 5
Sellers Have to Create Value, Too

It used to be enough for a seller to deliver on the value that mattered most to the buyer. If a buyer expressed a preference for "made in the USA" and the seller had products manufactured in America, the value was recognized and the solution was sufficient. As competitive pressures increased, marketers began adding value to incentivize buyers. In addition to meeting preferences like "made in America," companies began offering added value, everything from the old S&H Green Stamps to today's Box Tops for Education. For many years, programs and offerings like these ensured buyer loyalty, in B2C and B2B, too.

> **The first inklings of dissatisfaction can be traced back to a lack of value creation by the seller.**

This is not the case any longer. Today, the same buyer wants "made in the USA" plus the standard added value AND something more. The "more" is seldom defined. Buyers don't know exactly what they want, but they know what it is when they find it. Until they find it, they are always on the lookout for it.

For a seller, this is a precarious position. Providing a product but not fully satisfying the buyer opens a window of opportunity for competitors to swoop in and steal the business. This is not an empty alarmist threat. This is what buyers describe. Sellers need to be aware and vigilant to prevent this from happening.

What causes this buyer dissatisfaction? It isn't always attributable to price or product quality or corporate image. It isn't necessarily a lack of value or a deficit in added value. Oftentimes, it's a lack of value creation. Even when the reason given by the buyer for choosing another supplier is lower price, superior quality or more appealing brand… Even then, the first inklings of dissatisfaction can be traced back to a lack of value creation by the seller.

Creating Value

Creating value is not the same as adding value. The bar has been raised significantly by empowered consumers who are looking for better, more, different, special and unique.

Adding value is expected in the course of regular business, and it takes many forms like customer incentives, no-cost options, loyalty programs and giveaways. It involves taking something with a value and adding it on for the buyer.

Creating value goes further. It requires identifying what would be of value to an individual buyer and then finding or making a way for that unique value to be realized. Unlike added value, created value is original and unique to the one buyer it suits.

Buyer demand for value creation has come about through a trickle-down effect. Companies began focusing on value creation to meet shareholder demands as competition escalated for many industries in the 1970s and 1980s. Now, decades later, consumers have followed this same pattern of wanting more, and they want it to come directly from their sellers.

> **Unlike added value, created value is original and unique to the one buyer it suits.**

What makes this challenging for sellers is buyers don't directly ask for value creation. Most buyers don't even think in those terms. All they know is they want a little something more, something different from what everybody else is already getting.

Take a look at Illustration 3 to better understand the differences between value, added value and created value. Give yourself and your company a quick evaluation – what value are you delivering and which type of value could you increase?

3 Levels of Value

Value	Added Value	Created Value
The relative worth of a product based on utility and importance to the buyer	Extra features that go beyond the standard product offering.	Separate from the product and unique to each buyer.
Attracts buyer awareness and interest	Magnifies buyer desire and may lead to action.	Secures long-term buyer/seller relationships
Delivered by the product itself and how it meets the buyer's current needs	Delivered by the seller's company as a marketing tool to incentivize buyers and to gain a competitive edge.	Delivered by the seller through the experience created in doing business with the buyer.
All types of value must be relevant to the unique buyer. No value is "one size fits all."		

Illustration 3

Think about your own preferences as a buyer. If you were to shop in the same store on two different days, you'd expect the experience to be largely the same. Compare these two experiences:

Imagine on your first visit to the store you were browsing through a rack of clothing. A friendly salesperson approached and engaged in non-intrusive, helpful conversation. The seller asked what you were looking for, immediately understood what you wanted, and brought something from the back room that hadn't even been tagged for display yet. It was the perfect item, exactly what you'd hoped to find. You left the store, purchase made, feeling good about the transaction, the seller and the brand.

INSIDE THE SALES CALL

On a return visit to the same store, you enter with high hopes. You begin

35

browsing through the racks and notice the only salesperson in the store is standing behind the counter. She is having what seems to be a personal conversation on her cell phone. You feel a bit irritated. Soon, you find a very appealing clothing item, but it isn't available in your size. You approach the register, wait for the clerk's attention and ask if there are additional sizes in the back. The curt reply makes it clear the seller doesn't know, doesn't care and won't be checking in the back for you. You leave, disappointed, empty-handed and vowing never to shop there again.

> **We buy from people and businesses that make us feel good about the experience.**

The only difference in these two scenarios is what the seller created in the customer's experience. Same store, same merchandise, same pricing, same brand, same atmosphere… One could argue that buyers shouldn't expect anything more than what is on the racks or that it's unreasonable to expect personal service in a retail setting. Nevertheless, as empowered consumers, we have choices. We buy from people and businesses that make us feel good about the experience. We expect and respond favorably to value creation that personalizes our shopping experience.

We also buy from sellers who respect our time, the ones who don't waste a single minute on irrelevant pitches, mundane questions or rework. We appreciate when sellers are efficient, coming to meetings on time, prepared and fully engaged.

This doesn't mean buyers expect sellers to race through the agenda or to "take just a minute of your time" (as so many sellers promise when they book an appointment). What buyers want is to invest the right amount of time to get the value they need. If, within the allotted time, a seller also creates more value, the buyer feels the return on the time invested is even greater.

Creating value could be succinctly defined as taking the extra steps needed to let a buyer know he or she is appreciated. Some of the ways buyers report sellers have made them feel appreciated or special include:

- The seller took an extra measure of care to check a detail, make a call or follow through on something I was concerned about.

- The seller anticipated my needs, responding with ideas or asking questions I hadn't even thought of yet.

- The seller asked me about when and how to communicate with me and abides by the preferences I outlined.

- The seller took the time to explain how I could use her products and taught me about best practices in businesses like mine.

- The seller gave me advance notice about deadlines so I wouldn't have to make decisions at the last minute.

- The seller booked meetings directly on my Outlook calendar for me which was a big help because I was in between assistants.

- The seller tracked data and ran analysis for me so we could adjust order volume based on the early trend lines.

- The seller introduced me to someone and networked on my behalf to help me get a firmer foothold in the industry.

- The seller spoke my language and understood my business. We talked about what mattered most to me.

- The seller sent me articles and information pertinent to my business.

This is all easy to do! None of these examples take much time. Every one of these examples creates new value in the buyer's mind. Each of these seller's actions builds trust and loyalty. Asking quality questions pinpoints buyer priorities so sellers can create value.

What Prevents Value Creation?

Why don't more sellers create value in these simple ways that mean so much to buyers? After all, it seems to be common sense.

For sellers who carry heavy account loads, there is the multiplier effect to consider. Doing one of these things for one buyer is easy. Doing several of these for every buyer is abundantly more daunting. Sellers can have the best of intentions but then get caught up in the endless cycle of must-do work. Packing too many appointments and reports and tasks into every day just naturally results in trimming out the niceties. Unfortunately, this also means giving up the creation of value.

For sellers who focus on new business development, lead generation, prospecting and cold calling, there is often a mindset that more calls will lead to more sales. The "numbers game" may even be reinforced by call quotas or performance standards. Quantity over quality naturally results in trimming out time that could be spent on value creation.

For sellers who have been trained extensively on product features but never trained in fundamental selling skills (including the basic business acumen to understand the buyer's perspective), there is often no understanding of how or why to create value. Without even knowing it, these sellers may be leaving out the creation of value.

Whatever the reason, the result of not creating value is the same. The buyer/seller relationship is compromised. Buyers feel a vague sense of something missing. They feel marginalized instead of feeling special. Some even describe feeling "used" by sellers who rush impersonally through sales calls.

These feelings leave an opening for another seller, your competitor.

When buyers are dissatisfied, even vaguely, they are more likely to take calls from other vendors. Their interest and desire for something more can be piqued, and buyers may take action if the new seller creates the value that has been lacking in their interactions with you.

> When buyers are dissatisfied, even vaguely, they are more likely to take calls from other vendors.

The easiest way to prevent needless customer churn is for sellers to create value in every sales encounter by asking quality questions that engage buyers and make them think. Doing this displays a seller's genuine interest. Value is created, connections are made and sales advance.

CHAPTER 6
Seller Differentiation

Value creation goes hand-in-hand with competitive differentiation. You can't easily have one without the other. But competitive differentiation is increasingly difficult to achieve and communicate. Strong corporate brands aside, buyers think of similar products and companies as largely the same.

Competitive differentiation simply means a company and/or its products are different in some meaningful way from similar companies and products. The strategies used to achieve competitive differentiation include pricing, features, quality, selection, design, target market and more.

Being different isn't enough. Differentiation is only half the aim. Choosing the differences that will make a company and its products competitive is the real objective. That requires knowing what buyers value and then marketing to showcase how your differences deliver what is valued. Sellers must also be clear on the

> **Sellers must know how to position these differences to show, add and create value for each unique buyer.**

various ways their products are different. Sellers must know how to position differences to show, add and create value for each unique buyer.

It is more difficult to do this now than it was even a decade ago. True differentiation is not only more challenging to achieve, it is also more difficult to convey. Buyers, thanks to the broad access they have online to many other sellers, view products as commodities – as if one is just as good as the next.

At the same time, both buyers and sellers are busy. Both may overlook the need to talk about what makes a product or service different from all the similar ones available. Worse yet, many sellers have never even thought about this and cannot effectively answer the question "why should a buyer choose your product over a competitor's?"

Additionally, the needs assessment phase of a sales process is frequently shortcut as sellers race ahead to propose a solution. Without probing to understand what a buyer values, the best competitive differentiation the seller can offer remains generic and may be of low or no value to a particular buyer.

When all this is added together, the outcome is not surprising. But it is problematic for companies that need to maintain and grow market share. Without clear competitive differentiation, sales will not be as strong as they otherwise would be. Without clear competitive differentiation, over time a brand or company can become misunderstood, unappreciated and devalued.

Competitive differentiation is the responsibility of both the marketing department and the sales force. Ideally, there would be a cohesive message about what's different and why it matters to buyers. Marketing would promote those differences and would innovate and continually strive to keep products aligned with buyer demands. Sellers would build on these strategies to make the competitively differentiated features apparent to buyers. They would selectively present the ones which are most appealing to each buyer in a way that resonates with the individual buyer's primary value.

This doesn't always happen. When it does happen, sales grow. When it doesn't happen, sellers have to work even harder to retain each customer's business and to appeal to new prospects. Without clear competitive differentiation of products or brand, the seller must take an additional step.

Seller Differentiation

That extra step is for the seller to **personally** differentiate himself or herself from all the other sellers vying for the buyer's business. This is a best practice for sellers even when representing strong brands or products.

Some sellers retain customers singlehandedly. That's what's happening when buyers migrate to follow a seller who leaves an organization. Buyers choose the seller even though the company, brand or product is no longer competitively differentiated in the customer's mind. Every seller should strive for that kind of buyer loyalty by differentiating himself or herself.

Seller differentiation includes anything setting you apart in a way that makes you competitive. Without relying on your company's brand or your product's strengths, think about why a buyer would choose to do business with you personally. What do **you** bring that is of value?

As you consider this question, focus on what you bring with real, relevant and apparent value to the buyer. That you were the #1 seller in your company last year is simply not of value to the buyer. That you have more experience than most other sellers in your market and field is also not of interest to your buyer. In fact, both of these facts could be viewed negatively by the buyer. The top seller, the buyer may think, must be really aggressive and pushy. The most experienced seller, a buyer might assume, won't have any fresh or new ideas for us and will be stuck in the past.

Like competitive differentiation of your company or product features, what you present about your own differentiation must be of value to the buyer. As we've established, value is inherently personal. What this means is you must be different in multiple ways,

> **Seller differentiation includes anything that sets you apart in a way that makes you competitive. What do YOU bring that is of value?**

and you must be capable of expressing those differences in a way that is meaningful to each buyer.

The seller who has more experience than other sellers in the market, then, might consider expressing her distinction in various ways:

- For the buyer who is new to the industry, the seller would extend access to her extensive network.

- For the buyer who is also an industry veteran, the seller would leverage mutual connections and shared history.

- For the buyer who is creative and looking for new ideas, the seller would offer brainstorming sessions and bring in an alternative perspective for connecting resources and ideas.

- For the buyer who is cautious and slow to change, the seller would bring in testimonials from long-term, satisfied customers.

- For the buyer who is data driven, the seller would share research and tell the stories behind the numbers as only someone with an insider's perspective, experience and business acumen could.

The starting point for the seller is, of course, knowing which buyer she is working with each time. When sellers open with generic credentials, they take a risk and may negatively differentiate themselves. Starting instead by getting to know about the buyers, their perspectives, and what they will value keeps sellers' options open. It is impossible to tailor seller differentiation to the buyer until you know about the buyer.

Seller's Personal Brand

Seller differentiation also includes the seller's own personal brand. Intentional or not, every seller develops and telegraphs a brand. For some, the brand is highly polished and professional. For others, the brand may be free-spirited, flexible, approachable, customer-focused, creative, energetic, thoughtful or persistent. Some sellers communicate a brand that is flighty, disorganized, aloof, intense, distracted, desperate, rigid or pushy.

Personal brands are earned by the way a seller presents himself or herself to others. Without deliberate thought, conscious choices are not made about the brand. Instead, an accidental brand may be positive or negative. Either way, the seller's personal brand is another point of differentiation. In order to stay competitive, sellers are well-advised to manage their own brand and to act in a manner which conveys what they would like buyers to believe about them.

There may be times when a seller's brand is not aligned in some way with a company's brand. Companies may try to screen for abilities that will help maintain image alignment in their recruiting processes. Or they may have onboarding training for new hires to communicate what image is expected of sellers. For example, a seller selected to be an "Apple Genius" attends a 14-day training program. During this training, the people who will work at the "Genius Bar" in an Apple retail store are taught how to be empathetic and how to understand what customers need and want.

The desired brand, then, for this team is "understanding and empathetic." A seller who displays behaviors contrary to this image would be differentiating himself, but this would be in an unfavorable way because buyers have expectations related to their usual experience.

For sellers who want to extend or supplement the company or product differentiation, it is important to stay aligned with the established image and to also get aligned with what will be of value to each individual buyer. Both practices will ensure your differentiation is a competitive advantage rather than being ineffective or counter-productive.

Getting alignment, tailoring the way you position your competitive differentiation and creating value through your differentiation can be done best when you utilize questions. Building a brand and attempting to connect based on assumptions will do more harm than good. Instead, ask your buyers questions so you can understand them and position yourself to meet their needs in ways other sellers do not.

CHAPTER 7
Questioning with Strategic Intent

The first six chapters of this book have focused on understanding value, adding value and creating value. To meet buyer demands, sellers must start and end every sales encounter with value. Sellers do this by differentiating themselves, building trust and demonstrating to buyers how much they care. Each of these objectives has been linked to asking questions. To recap:

- Asking questions enables sellers to understand what buyers value.

- Asking questions reveals the hierarchy of buyer preferences.

- Asking questions builds rapport and trust.

- Asking questions improves trustworthiness and serves a specific purpose in all 12 Dimensions of Trust.

- Asking questions creates value for buyers challenged to think in new ways.

- Asking questions stimulates dialogue and signals the seller is genuinely interested in what matters to the buyer.

- Asking questions and gathering information about what matters to the buyer prepares the seller to position product benefits in a way that will be relevant and compelling.

- Asking questions keeps the seller and buyer processes aligned.

- Asking questions will help the seller to avoid making dangerous assumptions about the buyer's awareness, interest and desire.

- Asking questions creates new value and differentiates the seller who asks them from all other competing sellers.

Why Sellers Don't Ask Questions

There are right ways and wrong ways to ask questions. Savvy sellers know that ill-timed, awkward, and low-value questions are poorly received by buyers. That's why some sellers feel asking questions is too risky.

It magnifies the feeling of risk when a seller doesn't have business acumen about what it takes for buyers to be successful. Asking a question may trigger answers the seller won't understand. There is a fear of exposure if the conversation turns to something the seller is unfamiliar with, so sticking to talking points about his or her own product seems safer.

Along with an element of risk, there is also the constant time pressure for both sellers and buyers. Sellers may not see the value in inviting lengthy discussion, and they may believe buyers don't want to spend time answering questions either. They opt instead for the expedience of a generic product pitch.

Add to the mix that many sellers feel questions are intrusive, pushy or nosy. Some feel it would be downright rude to pry into the buyer's business. Some sellers believe they are on a "need to know" basis, and buyers will tell them whatever it is they absolutely must know.

Furthermore, questioning others tends to have negative associations attached to it. Words like interrogating, cross-examining, investigating and scrutinizing come to mind and then drum up imagined reactions like defensiveness or retreat. These hostile images of how people think of questions cause sellers to feel it is inappropriate to ask questions. Others avoid asking because they abide by the philosophy of the classic courtroom attorney who says "you should never ask a question unless you already know the answer."

Finally, since question-asking is a skill, but it's not formally taught in most circles, many people truly don't know the difference between a well-constructed question and an awkwardly phrased one. Even if they sense the difference as they ask the question, most people cannot pinpoint or explain the difference and cannot replicate a good question nor avoid asking an awkward one again.

> It's easy to understand why so many sellers shy away from asking questions!

It's easy to understand why so many sellers shy away from asking questions! It's risky, scary, time consuming, potentially rude, may be discouraged, and is an under-developed skill for most.

Despite all that, the case for asking questions is compelling. It's worth your time to fully develop the skill of asking effective questions.

This is hardly the first book or training program written for sellers to help them use questions as a tool for increasing sales. Extensive research has been done on the art and science of asking questions. Even with the plethora of materials available on this subject, many sellers haven't embraced questions. The aim of this book is to change how sellers view and use questions.

Sales training programs and books positioning questions as a tool to help sellers advance the sale tend to take one of three approaches:

1. They assign formulaic and/or scripted questions to various parts of the sales process. Some have created sales processes based on a construct of specific types of questions.

2. They provide lists of questions to be mixed and matched. These are designed to gradually corral the customer into a pre-determined solution.

3. They offer (sometimes complex) models for when to ask canned questions.

What these resources all share is an awareness of questions' abilities to dramatically increase a seller's effectiveness. But what many fall short of doing is to lay out both the why's and how's of question-asking so the methods prescribed are accessible by any seller in any sales situation. It's like the difference between giving a man a fish so he can eat today instead of teaching a man to fish so he can eat every day.

Making Your Questions Count

In the remainder of this chapter, along with chapters 8-11, sellers will be reminded of and introduced to the fundamentals of asking questions. Before moving into the specific types of DISCOVER Questions®, sellers should understand how and why to use questions. There's more to it than inserting an occasional question in a sales conversation. Instead, sellers should be strategic and deliberate with their questions in order to realize all the potential benefits of asking questions and to eliminate the perceived risks associated with asking questions.

Part of the challenge for sellers is in overcoming two mutually exclusive perceptions about questions. Believing that asking questions is so simple and natural that there's no need to learn how to ask them is one barrier. At the opposite extreme is the belief that asking questions buyers will respond positively to is so difficult it's not worth the time and effort.

> **Knowing where you want to go with your questions keeps you from meandering.**

Neither belief is accurate. While it is true we can all form and ask questions with relative ease, there is also room for improvement in the way we structure and sequence our questions. By being more thoughtful and strategic in crafting questions, sellers can create value for buyers and advance the sale.

Questioning with strategic intent simply means the seller has a plan. The questions asked are all purposefully linked to the seller's plan. This automatically eliminates a whole host of random questions that seem, to the buyer, like a fishing expedition. Knowing where you want to go with your questions keeps you from meandering and enables you to recognize which answers move you closer to your objective. Knowing the purpose of your questions gives you clarity about when to drill down for more information and when to change direction.

When a seller knows it is time to close the sale, for example, her plan should be to tie up any loose ends and go for the close. With this goal in sight, the seller would ask very narrow questions. The intent is to keep the sale advancing forward, not to open up entirely new discussion topics.

Narrow questions sound like this:

- Do you have any additional questions about our technical support before we come to an agreement?

- Which option are you leaning toward?

- When would you like to get started?

- Would you like for me to set you up on the auto-renewal program we discussed?

- Are we ready, then, to send this through to production?

When sellers are unclear about their own intent, the questions they ask are unfocused and can lead buyers astray. At exactly this same juncture, in a sale that's about to close, imagine what would happen if a seller asked these broad and vague questions instead of the ones above:

- So what do you want to do from here?

- What else do you need from me today?

- I was also curious about how you got started in this business.

- Do you have time for me to tell you about another option?

The second set of questions moves buyers away from, not closer to, the seller's goal. (By the way, these are all real questions asked during actual sales calls at times when a close seemed imminent.) Adrenaline-addled, these sellers spoke without first thinking strategically. Their questions were oddly timed, cost them the sale, and left buyers feeling confused.

INSIDE THE SALES CALL

Sellers have a reputation for "flying by the seat of their pants," and the idea of doing more planning may be unappealing for some. The good news is your preparation need not be long, involved or laborious. Planning for questions seldom requires much more than a quick internal check. The seller should be constantly checking and recalibrating in order to stay aligned with the buyer and to advance the sale as efficiently as possible.

To stay aligned, before asking their buyers questions, sellers need to first ask themselves:

1. Where is the buyer in the buying process?

2. Where am I in the selling process?

3. Are we aligned?

4. Where do I want to steer this conversation next?

5. What kind of question will take us there?

Initially, a seller will have to be disciplined to think through these five questions. But the conditioning of doing this consistently will turn it into an unconscious process which keeps sales on track.

In addition to having a plan mapping call objectives, sellers also need to have clear intent about what they want to accomplish. The plan plus the intent will work together to spawn appropriate questions.

This intent will be informed by the seller's own selling style and the company's sales culture. The seller who has an intent to "close at all costs" will do business differently and use questions differently than a seller who has an intent to build long-term client relationships.

For our purposes here, we'll focus on sellers who have an intent to build long-term relationships founded in trust and a desire to do what's right for the buyer.

Knowing and staying true to this intent will guide the questions you ask and the information you choose to probe. Your intention to fully understand your buyer's needs and create a solution to address those needs will, for example, lead you to a number of questions a seller who is in it for a one-and-done transaction would not ask.

Check Your Intent

Sellers who have a strategic intent to meet buyer needs will ask questions to uncover those needs. Sellers who plan to sell the same product with all the same specifications regardless of buyer needs shouldn't waste time with questions designed to understand buyer needs. There is no point in asking questions to yield information that won't be used.

By the same token, a seller who wants to understand a buyer's needs shouldn't abandon her intent at the first glimmer of a potential need. If the intent is truly to understand the need(s), there will be follow-up questions to probe the stated need and to ascertain the scope and hierarchy of each need. When sellers leap ahead, as if a Pavlovian response kicks in to sell at the first sign of opportunity, the intent they started with is lost. Their credibility is lost, too, if the intent to understand needs was communicated to the buyer.

Step #1, then, in questioning with strategic intent, is to formulate a plan. A seller should know his or her objective(s) for each call. The plan will guide the questions and keep you focused on your desired outcome.

Step #2 in strategic questioning is for the seller to be aware of his or her own intent in the call. The intent is not the same as the plan. Two different sellers could have two different intentions – one may be a transaction-based seller with no expectation of repeat business while the other may be a relationship-based seller who relies almost exclusively on returning customers. Both, however, may have a plan in their next call to close the pending sale.

Both steps #1 and #2 ought to be completed before the sales meeting begins. Of course, plans may need to flex or change during a sales call. Even so, it's best to go in with a clear direction in mind. This is more effective than pre-scripting the questions to be asked. If the plan and the intent are clear, the questions will be a natural outgrowth of them. Planning questions without having a roadmap or a compass is like setting out on a journey with only a few dollars in your pocket and no idea which direction to turn.

Step #3 for questioning with strategic intent is sharing the purpose of asking questions at the beginning of the sales call. This step alleviates seller apprehensions about asking questions and clues the buyer in to the purpose of the questions. One reason sellers get negative reactions to their questions is they jump right to a question without any set up or context. Caught unaware, buyers may be taken aback, puzzled or even defensive. These initial reactions make sellers reluctant to ask additional questions.

These buyer reactions are assuaged when the seller describes his or her intent for asking questions. The reason given to the buyer should be truthful and straightforward. Sellers should avoid overpromising. They should also avoid minimizing the process of asking questions. Don't say "I just have a couple of questions. It will only take a minute." Phrases like this diminish the value of asking questions. By setting a time limit, the seller is inadvertently instructing the buyer to keep it brief, too. That's exactly the opposite of what the seller needs to communicate.

To let the buyer know what is intended, a seller should use statements like these:

- "I'd like to start out by asking you some questions to better understand where you currently are and where you'd like to be in the future. When I understand your goals, I'll be able to offer a solution to support you in reaching those goals."

- "Your last order with us fell short of your expectations. I'd like to take some time to get realigned so we won't disappoint you again. I have several questions to clarify how things went wrong. With this information, I'll do what I can to resolve any lingering problems."

INSIDE THE SALES CALL

- "It's my intention to only offer you products that can help you achieve your goals or overcome your business challenges. It would be presumptuous for me to offer you anything without first learning more about your current needs. So I'd like to interview you and learn about your business needs."

- "I want to make sure we're on the right track. Rather than making assumptions, I'd like to check in with you on several key questions before we proceed."

- "I know how busy you are. Rather than wasting your time with irrelevant information, I'd like to get better acquainted with your preferences. With most of my clients, I find asking some preliminary questions when we get started saves us both a lot of time in future meetings. I'll be more effective and more efficient in delivering exactly what you're looking for."

These set-up statements are not apologetic. They are not designed to buy time or to manipulate the buyer in any way. The purpose of these statements is to explain the reason the seller will be asking questions. Nothing more and nothing less.

Having described the purpose of the questions that are about to be asked, the seller now has an obligation to live up to the stated intention. The seller is accountable to the buyer for remaining true to the promise made in the statement of intention.

Remember, buyers are conditioned to be skeptical of any promises made by sellers. They may expect sellers to ask gotcha! questions. If buyers are initially apprehensive, it is probably due to a fear they could be backed into a corner by your questions.

Any deviation the seller makes from the stated intention will signal insincerity and cause the buyer to withhold information. Since trust can be built by asking questions, sellers should be particularly careful to keep the commitments they made in the statement of intention.

Consider this example of a seller forgetting his intent:

Seller: "How many more contract clients do you hope to sign?"

Buyer: "Ideally, I'd add 10-12 to my current list."

Seller: "Well, I have a product for targeting physicians across the state. An ad campaign there would..."

INSIDE THE SALES CALL

This seller, just two questions into a needs assessment, heard a potential need from the buyer. Rather than proceeding with the needs assessment, the seller seized the perceived opening and jumped right into a sales pitch.

In addition to losing credibility and trust, this seller missed out on an opportunity to probe and learn more about the situation. Look what would have happened with just one more question:

Seller: "How many more contract clients do you hope to sign?"

Buyer: "Ideally, I'd add 10-12 to my current list."

Seller: "Tell me about your plans to add these clients."

Buyer: "I'm not there yet. Before I can add, I need to shore up and preserve the clients I already have. We've taken a blow to our image and I'm doing damage control..."

INSIDE THE SALES CALL

One additional question revealed an entirely different situation. The first seller's hasty solution clearly doesn't fit the situation and would not meet the buyer's need at all.

A seller who has an intention – a true one – to understand a buyer's needs before offering a solution will ask these kinds of follow-up questions. The intention is what produces the right questions. There is no substitute for intention. There is no pre-determined list of questions capable of masking true intention. Intent will show through. So think it through before defining it publicly. Once it's been expressed to the buyer, stick to it to maintain your credibility and to build trust.

> **The likelihood of making a sale increases when trust, credibility and relevance are established.**

For sellers who believe every hint of an opportunity should be immediately addressed, here are three reassurances to help you wait patiently before you shift into selling mode.

#1 Buyer needs do not evaporate in the course of a single sales meeting. Jotting down the clues you hear about potential sales opportunities will help you remember to come back to them after you've completed the interview or delivered on your stated intention. It is far better to come back to a potential buyer need than it is to pounce on one before you have all the information.

#2 The likelihood of making a sale improves when trust, credibility and relevance are established. Asking questions to reveal and understand the buyer's needs do exactly that – build trust, demonstrate credibility and ensure relevance. The process of asking more questions will likely increase, not decrease, the chances you have of making a sale. You will not lose the opportunity by waiting until you've asked a few more questions.

#3: Following through on what you promised and behaving differently from other sellers is a surefire way to create value. This is unexpected and refreshing for the buyer. Good questions make the buyer think. When you are the one asking quality questions and making the buyer think, you are the one creating value. This differentiates you from all other sellers.

Questioning with strategic intent takes practice. Planning makes questions more purposeful and focused. Setting an intention keeps a seller on track and in alignment with the personal brand he or she would like to portray. Communicating the intention to the buyer sets the stage for asking questions to understand buyer needs.

Practice, planning and deliberate focus on your own intention will pay off in improved relationships and accelerated sales.

CHAPTER 8
Question Construction

Determining a strategic intention for your questions will eliminate many of the common concerns sellers have about asking questions. You can also reduce the time it takes to ask questions and gather essential information by improving the way you construct your questions. Better questions yield better information. Getting better information with fewer questions means less time is spent.

An added benefit of thoughtful question construction is buyers will be more engaged during the time spent answering quality questions. Good question construction will make buyers think, challenging them to go beyond superficial or ready-made responses. Buyers who are challenged by their sellers in this way appreciate the process and say the sellers have created unique value.

To craft questions yielding the type of information the seller wants, the seller must first understand what he or she wants. This seems obvious, but it is a step that is skipped all too often (probably because it seems so obvious). Without this clarity, the questions a seller asks will not be as effective.

Questions Steer Conversations

For example, early in any sales process the seller will want to know what the buyer needs. Here are five questions, asked by five different sellers as the opening question in the needs assessment phase of a selling process:

1. What do you already know about our products?

2. Are you planning to make a switch or to supplement your buy?

59

3. What volume do you use in an average month?

4. What is your budget?

5. What are your top three goals for the new year?

All five sellers had been instructed to learn about their buyers' needs, and all five interpreted the instructions differently. Four of the five took a narrow view to ascertain the buyer's need for the product the seller wanted to sell. One asked about product knowledge. Three tried to get an idea of the scope of the opportunity related to market share, volume and revenue potential. Only one asked a question about a buyer's broader needs.

Each of these five questions yielded different information and set a different tone for the meeting. Since all five sellers had booked a 30-minute meeting and had already outlined their strategic intent by saying "I'd like to ask a few questions to learn more about your needs," the buyers were all equally prepared for the needs assessment interview. Even so, the calls were dramatically different. Here's how they played out:

Seller 1: "What do you already know about our products?"

The buyer's initial reaction was generous. She pulled out a file of information from her desk drawer, making it clear she had done her research before the meeting. She objectively described what she'd heard from others in her organization and mentioned some factoids like the year the seller's business was founded. Then she flipped the pages of her legal pad back to a list of concerns and objections she'd gathered. As she began rattling off "what she knew about the products," the seller became discouraged. He tried, just once, to redirect the conversation. But it was too late.

In the post-call debrief, the seller explained the choice to open with this question by saying "I didn't want to do a full-scale product pitch because I figured she already knew about some of our products. By figuring out what she already knew, I planned to limit what I pitched to whatever she still <u>needed</u> to know."

As a result of this experience, the seller's perception of questions was "questions are too risky." He repeated a common law school refrain: "you shouldn't ask a question unless you already know the answer."

In a post-meeting interview, the buyer said she thought the question was a bit odd. She felt the seller was expecting her to repeat the commercial messages about the company and perhaps do the selling herself. She also said she had not planned to share the list of others' concerns but did so because the seller asked.

Seller 2: "Are you planning to make a switch or to supplement your current buy?"

This buyer's initial reaction was defensive. Without hesitation he said "I'm not planning anything right now. I'm just doing my due diligence to see what's out there. I'm not about to make a move unless there's a good reason to do so. So far, I don't see a good reason." The seller was flustered by this response. He responded by attempting to provide some good reasons, going straight into a product pitch.

In the post-call debrief, the seller explained opening with this question by saying "There are some things I <u>need</u> to know before I can sell to any prospect."

As a result of this experience, the seller's perception of questions was "buyers don't tolerate questions."

In a post-meeting interview, the buyer said "I don't like being put on the spot. I don't even know this guy, and he's already trying to close me? I don't think so. I wouldn't mind answering a few questions, but I'm not that easy to sucker into a sale."

Seller 3: "What volume do you use in an average month?"

The buyer's initial reaction was to bring up a spreadsheet and cite a very specific number for the seller. Smiling and nodding, the seller said "That's good. You're right in the zone for me to handle your account. Let me show you…" From there, the seller began to pitch the product.

In the post-call debrief, the seller explained the choice to open with this question by saying "We have a Key Accounts team that handles larger volume accounts. If the lead is going to be above the limit, we <u>need</u> to know that right away and hand it off to the Key team."

As a result of this experience, the seller's perception of questions was unchanged. This is the same opening question he'd always asked. For him, the answer was either good news ("I get to work the lead") or bad news ("I have to turn over the lead"). This is a classic example of a seller who was utterly unable to put the needs of the buyer ahead of his own needs.

In a post-meeting interview, the buyer said "Why didn't he just ask me that question over the phone? If I wasn't 'in the zone' would he have packed up his bag and left me hanging? Or tried to sell me less than I needed? Somebody ought to tell the company that I don't really care about their processes. Leave me out of that juggling act."

Seller 4: "What is your budget?"

The buyer's initial reaction was to be offended by the question. He said "Seriously? You just met me and you're already reaching into my pocket?"

The seller defended his question by saying "I don't want to waste your time or mine, so I'm just trying to understand what we've got to work with." The buyer crossed his arms, refused to answer the question, and gave curt replies to the questions the seller asked next. It was a long 30 minutes because neither the sale nor the relationship took shape.

In the post-call debrief, the seller explained the choice to open with this question by saying "I <u>need</u> to manage my time. The more budget they have, the more time I will spend with them."

As a result of this experience, the seller's perception of questions was "some people won't answer questions because they feel sales questions are too intrusive."

In a post-meeting interview, the buyer said he would have waited to ask the budget question. He said he didn't mind the question, and he understood its purpose. But, he said, because it was the very first question asked the seller seemed greedy, as if he was evaluating the buyer "with dollar signs in his eyes."

Seller 5: "What are your top three goals for the new year?"

The buyer's initial reaction was to pause and think. Then she talked for a solid four minutes, giving details about history and present state and the vision for her department's growth. She was animated and expressive, pausing only when she observed the seller needing time to catch up in her note-taking. The seller asked several more questions, and the 30-minute meeting lasted an hour. Then the buyer and seller made plans to have lunch two days later so the seller could present some ideas back to the buyer.

In the post-call debrief, the seller explained her choice to open with this question by saying "I started off broadly to understand the overall <u>needs</u> of the business. That gave me context for why and how they may <u>need</u> my products. If I hadn't started with their <u>needs</u>, I might have missed something important."

As a result of this experience, the seller's perception of questions is they are absolutely essential. She described this sales call as her "best ever" and attributed the difference to her own strategic use of questions and her intent to truly understand the buyer's needs.

In a post-meeting interview, the buyer said "Wow! I wish more sales reps would do business so professionally. She really made me think and even if I don't buy anything it was totally worth my time. But don't worry! I plan to buy from her because she really gets me and knows what I'm looking for."

From these five example, it's easy to see how "understanding customer needs" is subject to a wide variety of interpretations. Sellers' needs also factor into the equation and blur the lines between the stated intention "to learn more about buyer needs" and the reality that sellers do need to manage their time and deal with internal issues like sales force structure.

Sellers' internal motivations or intentions push them to see the sales call in a certain way and to set objectives. From the intent, the view of the call, and the objectives, questions are formed or questions are set aside.

This is why getting the intent firmly established is a critical first step, as outlined in Chapter 7. The seller's intent shapes the construction of questions, both in their content and in their form.

Question Content

The content of a question isn't always easy for a seller to define. In the five examples offered above, each seller knew exactly why they asked the opening questions they chose. The first four were driven by their own needs or by their pre-conceived notions that the buyers needed their products. Their questions reflected the needs they were focusing on first.

Just as often, sellers do not know exactly why they are asking a particular question. Maybe it's because a seller is parroting a question he or she heard on a four-legged sales call with a manager or a question a co-worker asked over the phone or a question suggested in training or in a book on selling skills. Maybe it's just because they know they should ask questions. Or maybe it's because sales calls feel one-sided, and they would like to get their buyers talking, too.

Without understanding the strategic purpose of their own questions, sellers will sound scattered, and their questions will not make sense to buyers. Additionally, not grasping the strategic value of questions causes sellers to miss key information revealed in response to those questions. When sellers ask random questions with no clear direction, they talk over their buyers or ask multiple questions in rapid fire. This is confusing for buyers. For sellers, it is unproductive because the constant retooling of questions and attempts to recover from awkward questions take their focus off listening to the buyers' responses.

The dialogue below is a script from an actual sales call. After this call, the seller learned to think more strategically about how to craft questions and about the importance of understanding the intention behind each question. Building those skills made a huge difference in his sales interactions. As you read through the dialogue of the call, try to relate to what's happening. Look for parallels between what this seller is doing and what you may be doing in sales calls when you, too, lack clarity about what you'd like to know.

Seller: So… How long have you been in business?

Buyer: Next year will be our 10-year anniversary.

Seller: I bet the years have gone by quickly. Did you start the business?

INSIDE THE SALES CALL

Buyer: Yes. I had a partner at first.

Seller: Didn't work out?

Buyer: It was okay. I bought him out when he decided to move because his wife took a job in Cincinnati.

Seller: So now it's just you making all the decisions? Do you have any silent partners or other people involved?

Buyer: My management team makes a lot of the decisions. It just depends on the type of decision and what's involved.

Seller: So big decisions go up for a vote? I mean, let's say you were thinking about a change in suppliers. Would everyone be involved in that decision or would you just tell them? Is it all managers or certain managers?

Buyer: It really depends on...

Seller: *(Interrupting)* Like if you were thinking my company could be a good fit with your company... Then what? Who else would you be talking to about doing business with us? Should they be here now? Would it be better if I met directly with someone else?

Buyer: Since I don't know a lot about your systems, I can't answer that right now. I took the meeting to try and understand more about the full integration functionality you mentioned. We have some systems that work well, some that don't. The idea of full integration is appealing but could be overwhelming. I'm just looking to get a better sense of what's involved before I bring in anyone else.

Seller: Okay, I have some other questions, too, so let me just look at my list here... We don't really know who the decision makers will be. Next, um, could you tell me more about your budgeting processes and buying cycles?

Buyer: Yeah, sure. What do you want to know?

Seller: Well, budget process... And it says buying cycles... Let's just come back to that later.

Buyer: It's...

Seller: *(Interrupting)* I just don't feel right asking about that. Let's try this one. What is the lifetime value of a customer?

Buyer: Hmmmm... I'd have to do some calculations... That's a good question. Let me open up this referral data...

Seller: *(10 seconds later)* We can come back to that, too. I don't want to take up too much of your time. Who is your ideal customer? You know, the company size, geography or whatever...

Buyer: Right. Is it okay if I bring up a little data to answer that? We track it and it's the first of the month, so I've got the most recent report.

Seller: If you want, you can just send it to me.

Buyer: No, I can't send this. It's not something I want floating around.

Seller: I understand. So what is the average transaction for a sale?

Buyer: Do you want me to look that up?

Seller: Only if you want. You could just give me a ballpark number. I'm also wondering about frequency of transactions. Like how often does a customer purchase, I think?

Buyer: This is a lot of detailed information. Where are you going with this?

Seller: I'm just, uh, asking questions about your business before I tell you about my business. You know, to see the fit for both of us? To, um, uh, you know, help you make the right selection?

In this situation, the seller had been given a list of pre-written needs assessment questions. The seller had not been to a training program to learn the purpose or value of these questions. He didn't know what some of the questions meant, let alone how the information gathered could be used. Unfortunately, this is not uncommon. It is one of the reasons why sellers reject questions and the process of needs assessment.

Throughout this dialogue, the seller asked the questions and expected the buyer to provide instant answers. Presumably, the seller thought the value of the question would become apparent in the answer. When pressed to explain a question or the purpose of a question, the seller was unable to do so. The seller saw so little value in the questions that he did not allow time for the buyer to answer even when the buyer affirmed the question.

This seller did not understand the content of his own questions nor the intent behind them. Without clarity of intent, questions will not be crafted effectively. Without understanding the content you'd like to see in a response, you can't craft questions to efficiently yield that content.

Contrast these three question pairs to distinguish between the before and after versions of questions. The "before" questions were vague because the sellers weren't quite sure what they wanted to achieve. The "after" questions are better because the seller paused to get clarity.

INSIDE THE SALES CALL

Before: You've been with ABC Company a long time, right?

After: Tell me more about your history with ABC Company.

Intention: To understand the buyer's history and background, not merely to generate "small talk."

Before: Do you have any plans to expand in the near term?

After: What is your strategy in this market over the next 5 years?

Intention: To learn about the 5-year strategy in one market.

Before: How are we stacking up so far?

After: What will the deciding factor be in choosing a supplier?

Intention: To identify the top decision criteria in supplier selection.

Starting with the intention enables sellers to craft more effective questions, like the "after" questions shown here. Before you ask a question, ask yourself "what do I really want to know and why?" This mental exercise will instantly improve the questions you ask.

Once you pinpoint what it is you're interested in, your question will be more specific. The buyer's answer will give you the information you're looking for. You'll be less likely to belabor the interview with follow-up questions that go in endless circles. The construction of your question will yield the content you desire.

Question Form

In addition to aiming for specific content through question construction, sellers can also improve their effectiveness by paying attention to the form of their questions.

Questions take two forms. They are either open-ended or closed-ended. The difference between the two forms is closed-ended questions can be answered with a simple "yes" or "no" response while

> **Open-ended questions yield open responses.**

open-ended questions invite more than a "yes" or "no" answer. Each form has specific purposes.

The purposes for open-ended questions include opening up dialogue, soliciting wide-open responses, gathering information, and engaging the buyer. Open-ended questions yield open responses. They are useful during the needs assessment part of the sales process or any time the seller needs more complete information. They are not as useful when closing the sale.

The purposes for closed-ended questions include getting confirmation or verification, checking for understanding, and narrowing the seller's responses. Closed-ended questions elicit shorter and less-detailed responses than open-ended questions do. They are useful when closing the sale or wrapping up a part of the sale before moving to the next topic or phase of a sales process. They are not as useful in gathering information about buyer needs.

If you listen to the phrasing of questions throughout your day, you'll soon notice more questions are closed-ended than open-ended. In our day-to-day conversations, we tend to ask a lot of closed-ended questions. We do this even when we would like to have more than a "yes" or "no" reply. This is, in part, due to habit. It also occurs

> **The buyer may feel boxed-in by closed-ended questions.**

because some people feel closed-ended questions are more polite and less demanding than open-ended questions are. The third contributing factor to an over-abundance of closed-ended questions is most people will give a little bit more than a "yes" or "no" reply. So we mistakenly believe we've extracted complete responses when we have not.

In selling, too many closed-ended questions confine conversations.

Since the seller is going to ask a series of questions in a needs assessment process, crafting them in a closed-ended manner will sound like an interrogation. We give shorter answers in response to closed-ended questions. That means the volley of question/answer/question/answer will be rapid fire.

What's more, closed-ended questions suggest the person asking the questions is in a hurry. These clipped questions signal that only short answers are desired. The buyer may feel boxed in by closed-ended questions.

For sellers who push for a close too soon or lapse into product pitching before getting sufficient information from the buyer, there is another risk associated with closed-ended questions. They can seem like a blunt-force instrument if used to "tie down" the buyer. This selling technique was widely taught and used in the past. But in an age when buyers are empowered, fewer tolerate this approach.

Sellers should avoid using manipulative questions to try and fool a buyer into agreement. These methods almost always rely on closed-ended questions. For example, one outdated program suggests asking the buyer a series of seven questions. The first six should all be easy questions with clear "yes" answers such as "Do you want to succeed in business this year?" The seventh question is "Are you ready to sign with me?" The training claims the answer will be "yes" because the seller's first six questions supposedly conditioned the buyer to say "yes."

> **Using closed-ended questions in a needs assessment is like trying to shovel eight inches of snow off your driveway with a teaspoon.**

Closed-ended questions can be misused and misunderstood. But the biggest problem with closed-ended questions is they do not yield nearly as much information as open-ended questions. Closed-ended questions prevent sellers from gathering the information needed to truly understand buyers' needs.

Using closed-ended questions in needs assessment is like trying to shovel eight inches of snow off your driveway with a teaspoon.

Understanding the difference between open-ended and closed-ended questions is easier than developing the habit of asking more open-ended questions. Again, having the clarity of your strategic questioning intent will help guide the questions you craft. First, though, it's helpful to review the basics of questions form.

Familiarize yourself with the words on page 72 that lead into closed-ended questions and the ones used to pose open-ended questions, too.

Developing a discipline of deliberately crafting quality questions starts with being able to distinguish the starter words and what they will yield.

Closed-Ended vs. Open-Ended Question Construction

Closed-ended questions start with those pesky little words known as "helper verbs" or "auxiliary verbs." Every question beginning with one of these words can be answered with a simple "yes" or "no." Even when people politely answer with additional words beyond the "yes" or "no," they will be giving you less than they would give in response to open-ended questions.

Closed-Ended Question Starter Words:

Am	Are	Is	Was	Were	Have	Has
Do	Does	Did	Will	Would	Shall	Should
May	Might	Can	Could			

Open-Ended Question Starter Words:

Who	What	Where	When	Why	How	Which

You'll notice some of these open-ended question words invite short answers. That's okay. The object is to get something other than a "yes" or "no" response. When you ask open-ended questions, you invite buyers to think through their responses and give you complete answers.

To get the most information and provoke the most thought, sellers should also use command statements. Technically, these are not questions, but they serve the same purpose of inviting expansive responses. That's why I'll refer to them as questions throughout this book. Command statements should alternate with open-ended questions. Mixing them in adds variety and gives the seller a way to effectively and expediently draw out vital information. When you use a command statement, buyers will elaborate and give unabridged answers with lots of detail. These are highly effective questions to use when you probe buyer needs.

Command Statement Starter Words:

Tell me	Describe	Explain
Help me understand	Walk me through	Give me more detail
Take me through	Paint a picture	List

A seller can accidentally subvert the effectiveness of a command statement. If a helper verb is added before a command statement, it turns into a closed-ended question. This is a common mistake sellers make. "Describe your current constraints" will yield much more information than "Can you describe your current constraints?"

Look at these "before" and "after" questions to see how closed-ended questions have been retooled. The "after" questions yielded more information for the seller and were viewed by the buyer as more interesting, more thought-provoking and of higher value. In some cases, the open-ended questions also sounded less threatening to the buyers.

Before: Can you walk me through the new RFP process?
After: Please walk me through the new RFP process.

Before: Do you prefer a monthly billing cycle?
After: Tell me about your preferences for billing.

Before: Is this important to you personally?
After: How important is this to you personally?

Before: Does this concern you?
After: What about this concerns you most?

Before:	May I ask about your budget?
After:	What is the budget that's been allocated to this project?
Before:	Were you interested in seeing any other options?
After:	What additional options are you interested in seeing?
Before:	Would you describe your preferred customer?
After:	Describe your preferred customer.
Before:	Is quality the reason you are looking for a new vendor?
After:	What led you to look for a new vendor?
Before:	Are you the sole decision maker?
After:	Who else will be consulted in making this decision?
Before:	Wouldn't you like to increase your productivity?
After:	What goals do you have in relation to productivity rates?

The "after" questions are broader, more inviting and less restrictive than the "before" questions. By turning closed-ended questions into open-ended ones, sellers have a better chance of getting high levels of buyer engagement and more information.

The closed-ended questions aren't bad questions. In fact, some of them may be preferred to their open-ended alternatives. That would depend entirely upon what the seller wanted to achieve. If a seller only wants a narrow bit of information such as confirmation, then a closed-ended question like "Do you prefer a monthly billing cycle?" is appropriate. Knowing the difference in question construction plus having a clarity of purpose for your questions helps you achieve what you want.

Questions Put You In Control

By thinking strategically about questions and deliberately choosing the content and form of each question, a seller maintains tight control over a conversation with a buyer. It's as if the seller is in the driver's seat, steering the conversation.

The seller, as a driver would, knows the destination and is following a purposeful route to reach that destination. The buyer's response to each question may lead to a detour or may add some unexpected construction delays or scenic outlooks to the drive. But with the destination in mind, a seller won't view those responses as roadblocks. The driver doesn't hand the steering wheel over to the passenger when the road gets bumpy. Instead, at those times, the driver grips the wheel even tighter and focuses more on making the drive as smooth and safe as possible.

What gives the seller this level of control and confidence? Questions – not just any questions, but strategic questions based on the seller's pre-determined intent.

Although the seller, like the driver, is in control, strategic questions also benefit the buyer. Like a passenger, the buyer gets transported somewhere new. The passenger must trust the driver in order to settle in for the ride. Questions build trust even as the journey is beginning. Questions engage the buyer and stimulate thought-provoking discussions. This is high value for the buyer and helps the seller to stand out, favorably differentiated from all other sellers. With questions, the seller and buyer stay aligned in their processes just like a driver and a passenger would travel together if they were in the same vehicle.

Sellers who believe asking questions would be too risky and sellers who think questions disempower them have not taken these important steps:

1. Being aware of the 12 Dimensions of Trust and understanding how every aspect of trustworthiness is enhanced by asking quality questions.

2. Working to understand buyers before trying to make buyers understand the product offering.

3. Considering the buyer's process and aligning the sales process with it.

4. Understanding the inherently personal nature of value and probing to understand the unique value and its weight for each buyer.

5. Learning how to create unique, relevant and meaningful value for each individual buyer.

6. Differentiating themselves by focusing on their personal brands.

7. Formulating a plan for each interaction with buyers.

8. Determining the strategic intent behind questions in accordance with the plans set for sales calls.

9. Sharing strategic intent with buyers before asking questions.

10. Constructing questions so the content and form of each question will yield information desired by sellers **and** create value for buyers.

These ten steps represent the mindset, preparation and knowledge a seller needs in order to be effective in uncovering essential information. Skipping any one of these steps will diminish the seller's effectiveness with questions and may have domino effect results, too, that preclude establishing trust and building value through competitive differentiation.

In Chapters 9-11, sellers will be introduced to the next steps that further maximize the yield of each question and help sellers gather actionable information to advance every sale.

CHAPTER 9
Conversational Flow

Sellers who are prepared to ask strategic questions have a distinct advantage over those who are not prepared. Knowing how to construct quality questions and having a clarity of strategic intent underlying the questions puts a seller into the driver's seat, able to steer any selling conversation.

Maintaining control during the conversation requires mastery of a few additional skills. Like the skill of crafting strategic questions, these are not skills taught in school or in basic sales training programs. These are skills most hiring managers assume sellers walk in the door with and are able to put into immediate use.

This prevalent assumption can be linked to stereotypes painting all sellers as gregarious social types. People with the "gift of gab" may talk a lot, but even some talkative types lack the skills required to maintain strategic control of a conversation.

Maintaining control of a conversation in order to steer it to the places where information can be gathered and sales can advance goes well beyond basic socializing. A seller may be quite comfortable conversing in a casual setting, telling stories that engage others and being the "life of the party." But the same seller may struggle when it comes to moving a sales conversation from one question to another or from one phase of the selling or buying process to the next.

The skills needed are not entirely different. But the skills accessed must be prioritized and used in different ways. Let's look at the similarities.

First, selling conversations are just that. Conversations. A conversation is defined as an "interchange of thoughts and information through oral communication." A breakdown of this definition includes these key points:

- Interchange involves both parties.

- Thoughts and information include more than cold, hard facts.

- Communication includes transmitting **and** receiving. Both parties share, listen, process and reciprocate so thoughts and information can be exchanged.

- Oral means there is talking (not just an e-mail exchange!).

As simplistic as these key points may seem, they are extremely important to grasp. Not every seller abides by these basics when the sales call begins. Some forget it's a conversation. They may even try to dodge the two-way interchange in favor of just getting through the sales pitch. Or they may forget communication involves listening **and** responding because they are so intensely focused on transmitting information.

> **Selling conversations are just that. Conversations.**

The second way sales conversations ought to be like any other conversation is they should flow naturally. In normal conversations, an idea or question is offered. A response is given. Something within the response prompts feedback or a follow-up question. One idea flows into another, and the smooth course of the conversation is natural.

Sales conversations aren't always smooth. The reasons they do not flow naturally include:

- The seller is hyper-focused on a list of questions or on a pre-set agenda. The emphasis seems to be on making it through the list without regard for the underlying purpose of any one question or item on the list.

- The seller is afraid of objections, new information, questions she might not be able to answer, unfamiliar topics and/or of losing the buyer's interest. She tries to constrain the scope of the conversation so it doesn't get uncomfortable for her.

- The seller is painstakingly conscious of the time. He starts by apologizing for taking the buyer's time. He prefaces questions with minimizing statements like "I know you're busy, but if I could bother you for just one more minute…" He checks his watch frequently.

- The seller is unable to resist the urge to sell. Something! Anything! Right Now!

- The seller is speaking in a language the buyer doesn't understand or doesn't want to understand, using industry jargon or talking about product specifications that are too technical, irrelevant or low value for the buyer.

What's unfortunate about these awkward conversations is they happen with such regularity that buyers have come to expect little more when they meet with sellers.

This is one reason buyers are reluctant to set appointments with sellers and buyers choose automated ordering systems rather than working directly with sellers. No one wants to engage in an awkward, unnatural conversation. Sellers who take a more natural

> Staying in the moment means paying attention to right here, right now… giving full attention to the conversation, the speaker, the setting and the connection.

approach and have regular conversations – interchanges of ideas with two-way communication – clearly have a better shot at connecting with buyers.

There are two more ways regular conversations and sales conversations are similar. Both require sellers to loosen up and focus on what's happening in the conversation instead of focusing on the sale they hope to make. In casual conversations, it's natural to "stay in the moment" and to sequence questions logically, starting with broad topics and narrowing the focus as the conversation progresses. Sales conversations shouldn't be any different.

Staying in the Moment

As with any conversation, a seller should stay in the moment. Staying in the moment means paying attention to right here, right now. It means giving full attention to the conversation, the speaker, the setting and the connection.

Staying in the moment is impossible unless a seller eliminates all distractions and focuses completely on the buyer. This includes eliminating intrusive mental distractions about closing the sale, the next appointment, the looming quota, the possible objection the buyer may offer, and so on. It means turning off the cell phone and dedicating time and attention to the buyer (who expects no less).

Staying in the moment applies for both in-person and telephone meetings. Sellers who meet by phone may be surprised to learn buyers are extremely adept at identifying when a seller is "multi-tasking" instead of focusing on the phone conversation. Even the most mindless occupations like playing an online game during a phone call (yep, some sellers really do that!) prevent a seller from staying in the moment.

Why does staying in the moment matter so much? In addition to being a professional courtesy and part of a seller's personal brand, staying in the moment enables a seller to pick up on important clues offered by the buyer.

Distracted sellers miss all sorts of signals. Sometimes buyers' signals are subtle, like leaning in and paying closer attention. Sometimes the signals are spoken, like a question indicating genuine interest. Sometimes the signals are more in how something is said rather than being in the words themselves – a more serious tone or an enthusiastic response, for example. A seller who is not in the moment could miss all sorts of buyer clues.

It's not just the subtle clues distracted sellers miss. As you read through this dialogue from an actual sales call, put yourself in the seller's shoes. She was pressed for time, on deadline, running 20 minutes late for her next appointment and within striking range of making quota with two days left to go. This call was the sixth she'd made to a buyer who seemed condescending and unmovable. The seller was convinced the buyer took these appointments just for the amusement of giving her a hard time.

Seller: I wanted to bring you the analysis report we discussed when we met last week. It's hot off the press, and it validates the preliminary findings. This treatment eliminates 2.2% more impurities than our competitor's does.

Buyer: That is very interesting. Very interesting. *(Scanning the report.)*

INSIDE THE SALES CALL

Seller: I know you're already contracted through the end of next year…

Buyer: *(Interrupting.)* Please give me a minute.

Seller: *(Impatiently tapping pen, waits 40 seconds.)* I will leave the report with you if you'd like.

Buyer: *(Keeps reading, no comment.)*

Seller: *(Stands up, reaches for her bag.)*

Buyer: We'd have to go through legal, but I'm certain we included a clause that gives us an out if something like this happens.

Seller: *(Looks confused. Checks her watch.)* How about giving me a call after you read the report?

Buyer: I've seen what I need to know.

Seller: Okay. Then I guess I'll take that with me. Thank you for your time today.

Buyer: No. I need to keep this for our legal team.

Seller: Your legal team?

The seller completely missed the buyer's clearly stated interest and was prepared to leave with nothing. It's a good thing the buyer was so motivated. She patiently explained herself... This was a $2.5 million dollar sale in the making. By not staying in the moment, the seller nearly lost the sale.

When a seller focuses on what's happening here and now, he also allows his own natural curiosity to enter into the conversation. Being genuinely interested in and curious about what the buyer shares will serve a seller well. But it's impossible to be curious when your mind is wandering or is solely focused on closing the sale.

Being curious and interested leads to more natural conversations. A seller who doesn't let the conversation flow naturally, due to a lack of interest or curiosity, comes across like this:

Seller: What's your top priority for the coming year?

Buyer: I really need to focus on making the business as strong as possible. The day's coming when I'll need to put it on the auction block.

Seller: What was your profit margin last year?

Buyer: We came in right at plan, just under 12%.

Seller: Good to hear. What's the next big thing for you?

INSIDE THE SALES CALL

Buyer: Well, like I said, I'll be getting ready to sell out soon.

Seller: Any change in operations planned for this year?

By contrast, a seller who responds naturally picks up on the significance of what's been said and asks follow-up questions, conveying interest. These follow-up questions come easily to a seller who is curious. When a buyer says the business is up for sale, all sorts of questions leap into the curious mind – when? why now? how? what's involved?

> **Asking follow-up questions uncovers additional needs and more selling opportunities**

Not responding with interest and curiosity makes a conversation seem one-sided. There may not be an immediate selling opportunity apparent. But ignoring what matters to the buyer will impair trust, diminish value and plant a festering seed of dissatisfaction in the buyer's mind.

Asking follow-up questions uncovers additional needs and more selling opportunities. At a minimum, the seller who shows interest will build trust and gain competitive differentiation. Beyond that, there are also greater benefits to be realized in terms of more sales.

Proper sequencing of questions helps sellers progress from broad to narrower information. Follow-up questions facilitate the progression.

Sequencing Questions

It may help for sellers to think of a conversation with a buyer as moving through an inverted funnel, as shown in Illustration 4. At the top, questions are open-ended and very broad. They are about the business needs and the buyer's needs (not about the narrower needs for your product). Each follow-up question narrows the broad response and steers the

> **Proper sequencing of questions helps sellers progress from broad to narrower information.**

conversation. As warranted, a broad question may come back into the conversation in response to an answer given by the buyer.

Proper Sequencing of Questions

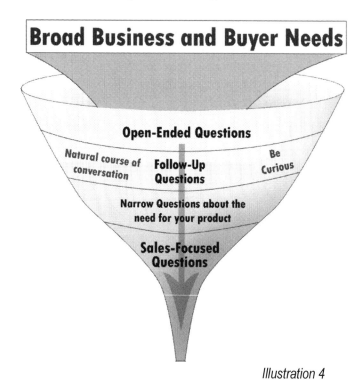

Illustration 4

By strategically crafting questions that yield responses with varied content and by using appropriate forms of questions, the seller can learn all the angles of a situation as it becomes better defined. As the seller gets to a point of fully understanding the buyer's priority, the conversation has narrowed to the end of the funnel. At this point, it is appropriate for the seller to hone in on the buyer's need for the seller's products.

Follow-up questions help the buyer, too. In a hurry-up world, taking time to fully consider one's own problems and what to do about them is something of a luxury. A buyer who is guided through this process gets value from the process alone. Quality questions make the buyer think, promote self-discovery and surface latent needs which may also need to be addressed.

Buyers appreciate sellers who can conduct a conversation leading to this type of helpful outcome. They also enjoy the conversations when sellers stay in the moment, show genuine

> **Follow-up questions help the buyer, too.**

interest, allow for a natural dialogue, sequence questions sensibly, and invite an interchange of ideas and information.

That's why strategic questions advance the sale and make the seller who uses them the one seller buyers really WANT to talk to.

CHAPTER 10
Questions to Avoid

Not all questions are created equally. Even with a pure and clear intent to focus on customer needs... even with an ability to ask well-constructed, strategic questions... even with an awareness of how to stay in the moment and conduct a natural conversation... even with all of this, sellers sometimes ask questions that cause buyers to mistrust them.

As a buyer, you probably consider the questions asked by some sellers to be manipulative. As a seller, though, you may ask those very same kinds of questions. This happens when we allow our misplaced perspective to supplant our good judgment and broader goals.

When sellers look at sales opportunities solely through the lens of selling, they over-focus on commissions and quotas. They think short-term and picture buyers as prey. This mindset changes the way they talk to buyers because it changes the way they view them.

> **Sellers sometimes ask questions that cause buyers to mistrust them.**

It's also possible to over-compensate. Sellers who only think long-term and look exclusively through the lens of the buyer's perspective also limit their own effectiveness. They become pro bono consultants instead of sellers, meeting to discuss the buyer's business but never advancing the sale.

Sellers need to wear bifocals so they can focus on both perspectives. Building trust and being interested in buyer needs cannot happen when a seller is singularly focused on making an immediate sale. At the same time, sellers cannot focus exclusively on customer consultations. Sellers must meet their buyers' needs **and** sell their own products. Being near-sighted or far-sighted compromises a seller's effectiveness. This often shows in the poor quality of questions a seller is asking.

There's only one way for a seller to strike a balance between buyer needs and seller needs. That perfect balance is reached when a seller understands the needs of the buyer so the solutions offered meet the needs of the buyer. Questions that probe to understand the buyer's need will enable this delicate balance. They will also build trust because they will simultaneously reveal the seller's intent.

At the needs assessment phase of a sales process, any other questions will do more harm than good. When is the needs assessment phase?

If the seller is aligning his or her selling process with the buyer's process, the seller will return to the needs assessment phase every time the buyer becomes aware of or interested in a new product, another feature, different options, or any other change. Because buyers' needs change (and their value hierarchy changes, too), strategic sellers should check in on buyer needs on a regular basis.

What this means to sellers is they need both an ability and a willingness to remain focused on buyer needs. This intent cannot be temporary or occasional. It needs to be a guiding light at all times. When it is, questions that engage the buyer and create value will naturally follow.

5 Question Types to Avoid

When the seller forgets or sets aside the intention to understand buyer needs, he or she asks different kinds of questions. It is apparent with those questions when the seller has become self-focused. Buyers describe these questions as low value, time-wasting, off-putting and offensive.

There are five kinds of manipulative-sounding questions sellers should avoid. If you hear yourself asking these types of questions, check your intention. Chances are a recalibration of strategic intention will help you get back on track with more productive and more effective questions.

#1: Avoid Asking "If I Could..." Questions

This commonly used technique is an obvious set-up. The seller asks the buyer a question to fabricate a conditional commitment. Then the seller proceeds to deliver on the condition he or she set up for the buyer with an expectation the buyer will proceed.

When the sale is nearing the close or in response to a sales objection, this can be an effective technique. But sellers should avoid slipping into this technique earlier in the sales process when their intent is to understand buyer needs. These questions do not reveal needs. They only reveal buyer responses to if/then scenarios.

There is a risk a buyer will feel manipulated at any stage of the sales process where this technique is used. Sellers should proceed with caution if they choose this phrasing or this technique. It is commonly used and is, therefore, familiar to buyers. Additionally, it feels like a trap and may cause buyers to put up their defenses. Sellers should evaluate their intent before using this technique, and they may wish to use a straightforward statement in these situations rather than setting up an if/then condition.

Examples of "If I Could..." questions include:

- If I could save you time, you'd be interested, right?

- What if I could show you how to get out of that contract?

- If I could match the price would you buy from me?

In some cases, a straightforward statement will serve the seller better. Rather than asking a hypothetical "If I Could" question, a seller can choose a statement like "I believe I can match that price and eliminate your concern about moving forward." This conveys the seller's intention and more efficiently moves the sale forward.

An assumptive statement like this is, in essence, what the seller who asks an "If I Could" question is telling the buyer. The subtle difference is there is no pretense of a condition and no perceived attempt to back the buyer into a corner.

One buyer said it this way "If you can, just say so."

#2: Avoid Asking Leading Question with Obvious Answers

If everyone already knows the answer, what's the point of asking a question? Sellers celebrate when they get the expected answer to questions like "Would you like to save money on your insurance premiums?" But a "yes" response to that simplistic question isn't a green light to a sales pitch. It's just a throwaway answer to a throwaway question.

"Wouldn't you agree that…" questions fall into this category, too. Some sellers put a lot of stock in these questions, and some deliver these questions with an intensity that is almost comical. Maybe you've been a buyer and seen this demonstrated by a seller. The seller locks into a penetrating gaze, begins to nod slowly as if trying to hypnotize the buyer and then asks, in a very serious tone, something like this: "Wouldn't you agree it's important to do the right thing for the people here who are counting on you?"

Who would say "no" to a question like that? At the same time, who would be compelled to buy as a result of such a leading question that adds no value and over-reaches? Frankly, the seller still has a lot of work to do to fill in the gap and explain why the "right thing" requires his or her product.

The problem with these types of questions is they annoy buyers. They are obviously leading, and no one wants to be led by a self-serving seller (and until the buyer's needs become the main topic, *all* sellers seem self-serving!). Also, these questions are not genuine. They don't provoke thought. They are usually answered with a "yeah, but" response, so they actually invite objections.

Sellers over-rely on leading questions with obvious answers because they misunderstand their own role. The job of a seller is not to manipulate, fool, lead, push or cajole a buyer into buying. The job of a seller is to sell. The most effective way to sell is by meeting buyer needs. Questions like this do not reveal buyer needs and are not effective in spotlighting how a seller can uniquely meet a buyer's needs.

#3: Avoid Asking Shame Questions

Questions meant to shame or embarrass the buyer into buying are strong-arm tactics and make the seller look like a schoolyard bully. In the age of empowered buyers, this tactic is outdated and unprofessional.

The apparent intention of these questions is to force the buyer to make a purchase out of a sense of shame or embarrassment. Even if this works to close a sale, the relationship between buyer and seller will be strained. What's more, the seller's brand and the company's reputation could be compromised. When buyer's remorse sets in, look for high rates of cancelled orders, dissatisfied customers and negative word-of-mouth reviews.

Like the other types of questions sellers should avoid, this one drives the seller's agenda without regard for the buyer's need. A seller who has conducted a thorough needs assessment, understands the buyer's need, and offers a solution that meets the stated need does not need to use a tactic like this. As the sale advances to a close, the seller who loses sight of the strategic intention and "goes in for the kill" risks undoing all that good work.

Examples of Shame Questions include:

- Oh, so you can't actually afford to buy this?

- Are you saying you don't have the power to make this decision on your own?

- If you weren't serious about this, why did you take this meeting?

These questions are often followed by a strong statement like "My time is valuable, too" or "I guess I was wrong about you." These digs are apparently meant to intensify the guilt the buyer is supposed to feel for not buying on the seller's timeline.

Needless to say, these questions and statements are manipulative and don't fit in with a strategic intention built on demonstrating trustworthiness and creating value.

#4: Avoid Asking Trite and Overused Questions

To the buyer, these kinds of questions seem manipulative just because they've heard them from so many sellers. The questions themselves are not necessarily meant to manipulate or lead a buyer. But they've been so often asked in an insincere manner that buyers assume sellers are not really interested in their replies.

Oftentimes, sellers who ask these questions don't know where to go next. That's a big part of the problem. When you ask how someone is doing, get a reply (sometimes including personal information), and then launch into a sales pitch, it seems like you don't really care what was shared. It's better to avoid asking a question if you don't intend to respond to what you hear.

> It's better to avoid asking a question if you don't intend to respond to what you hear.

Trite and overused questions set the bar low for both the seller and the buyer. Disingenuous opening questions set the tone for the rest of the meeting. A seller who starts with a low value throwaway question has to work harder to re-engage the buyer with the next questions. The time wasted on the meaningless questions plus the recovery time to re-engage the buyer could have been better spent.

Examples of Trite and Overused Questions include:

- How's everything going?

- What keeps you up at night?

- What will it take to get your business today?

Sellers who want to create value and differentiate themselves will recognize that hackneyed questions have no place in their conversations with buyers. The object is to engage buyers with a natural conversational flow. These questions aren't engaging because they're not natural.

#5: Avoid Asking Questions that Set Up Your Pitch

Another well-known manipulative technique starts with an attention-getting statement followed by a gotcha! question. But even when these are effective in getting buyers to tune in initially, buyers will quickly tune out once they realize they've been duped.

Examples of Set-Up Questions include:

- The Bush era tax cuts are about to expire. Have you taken steps to protect your family's income?

- Most mid-size companies are saving big money on data storage options they don't want smaller companies to know about. How'd you like to hear about their secrets?

- One in ten families declares bankruptcy within three years after the head of the household dies. What will happen to your family if you die unexpectedly?

What follows these questions will, of course, be a generic pitch about the product the seller has to offer. The opening gets the buyer's attention, so the seller goes full steam ahead into the pitch. The buyer's interest wanes as the pitch drones on. The realization soon hits. The question was just a generic set up; the seller led the buyer into an open trap. Feeling foolish, the buyer retreats.

Selling or Manipulating?

With these five types of questions, buyers react negatively because they feel sellers are trying to manipulate them rather than influencing or persuading them. Consider the difference in what these words mean to understand why manipulative questions push buyers away.

- to **Sell** means to induce or persuade someone to buy.

- to **Persuade** means to prevail on, urge or convince.

- to **Influence** means to affect, sway, move or impel.

- to **Manipulate** means to adapt, change or influence to suit one's own purposes.

The difference with manipulation lies in "to suit one's own purposes." Remember, buyers are wary when dealing with a seller. It doesn't take much for a seller to stoke the perception that he is self-serving. Sellers

> Sellers who appear to be focused on suiting their own purposes will find it far more difficult to establish trust and make sales.

who appear to be focused on suiting their own purposes will find it far more difficult to establish trust and make sales. Buyers can't be bothered with products, processes or people that don't deliver real value.

When sellers cross the line from selling, persuading or influencing into manipulating, buyers retreat. If sellers keep a pure intent to understand buyer needs and avoid these five types of manipulative questions, they will advance their sales more effectively and more efficiently.

Questions to Use with Care

There are four additional types of questions sellers should use with care during the needs-assessment phase of their sales process (or any time buyer needs are being re-examined). To err on the side of caution, sellers should consider their own strategic intent before asking these types of questions.

1.   Closed-Ended Questions

As described in Chapter 8, closed-ended questions do have very specific purposes in selling to confirm or verify information. Asking a closed-ended question closes a topic and enables the buyer and seller to move on to the next one.

Closed-ended questions can be answered with a simple "yes" or "no" reply. They start with helper verbs like am, is, did, can, and have. They do not stimulate thought or yield long, involved answers. For this reason, they are less valuable to a seller who is working to understand buyer needs. They do not create value for a buyer who is interested in being challenged or for one who is looking for a seller's help in sorting out the best solution.

When asked in rapid succession, a number of closed-ended questions will sound like an interrogation. The volley of questions and short replies can seem intrusive and may cause a buyer to wonder about the seller's intention. Additionally, closed-ended questions do a poor job of conveying curiosity and make it difficult for the seller to peel back layers of buyer needs for deeper level understanding.

For the seller who intends to fully understand buyer needs, closed-ended questions are much weaker than open-ended questions and command statements. Remember, open-ended questions start with who, what, where, when, why, which or how. Command statements start with "tell me more," "describe," "explain" and similar phrases.

2.   Sales-Focused Questions

Questions that inquire about how the buyer would use the seller's product can easily become overly focused on making the sale. Proceed with caution when asking these kinds of questions. The time for these questions is after the seller fully understands the buyer's broader needs. When a seller opens with sales-focused questions, the buyer will pull back. That's why sellers should avoid asking these questions too early in the sales process.

Sales-focused questions take many different forms. The best way for a seller to ascertain whether a question is buyer-focused or sales-focused is to check his or her own intention. Asking "will this question reveal buyer needs?" can help a seller be more discerning.

Questions about a buyer's broad needs should precede questions about the buyer's needs for the seller's products.

Sellers should think of this progression as an inverted funnel. At the beginning are broad, open-ended questions focused exclusively on the buyer's needs. As those needs become apparent, the funnel begins to narrow and the questions do, too. That's when the seller shifts to questions which reveal how the buyer's needs may be met by the seller's product. Finally, at the very narrowest point of the funnel, as the seller is beginning to see a clear solution for the buyer's needs, then (and only then!) the seller's questions become focused on the sale.

Another way of looking at this would be to overlay the question sequence funnel with the buyer's process. The process of buying starts with gaining awareness and then developing an interest. Only a buyer who is aware and interested will desire a product and take action to acquire it. Broad questions focusing on the buyer's need will open the buyer up to ideas the seller offers later because trust will develop and the seller will be differentiated. Interest grows when a buyer sees relevance and benefits. Sellers can only show relevance and benefits when they understand their buyers' needs clearly.

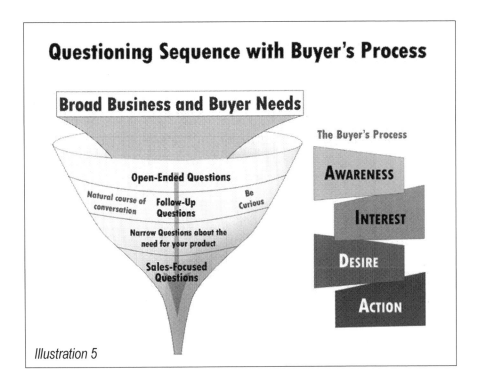

Questioning Sequence with Buyer's Process

Broad Business and Buyer Needs

The Buyer's Process

Open-Ended Questions

Natural course of conversation

Follow-Up Questions

Be Curious

Narrow Questions about the need for your product

Sales-Focused Questions

AWARENESS

INTEREST

DESIRE

ACTION

Illustration 5

When sellers skip ahead to sales-focused questions, they are at risk of losing sales for two primary reasons. First, the sale is jeopardized when a seller offers a solution that isn't quite right for the buyer. By making assumptions about buyer needs and skipping questions which would reveal more about those needs, the seller misses the mark.

Second, the sale is less likely to close when the buyer doesn't feel connected to the seller or to the solution. The process of asking questions about buyer needs not only reveals the needs but also builds trust, creates value, differentiates the seller, and facilitates a connection between the buyer and the seller.

Keep the visual of a funnel in mind as you contrast the kinds of questions to be asked at the beginning, middle and end of a needs assessment. Here are examples of questions to illustrate sequencing in alignment with the buyer's process.

Questions focused on a buyer's broadest needs (at the top of the funnel) sound like:

- What goals have you set for the coming year?

- What is your top priority?

- Tell me about your expansion plans.

- What is the impact if these goals are not achieved?

- How does this year's growth compare to last year's?

Questions focused on a buyer's narrower need for a seller's product (lower in funnel) sound like:

- What is your current volume and who supplies you now?

- What gaps in supply have you been experiencing?

- How do you measure the ROI?

- By not making a switch, what will the impact be on sales?

- How does the ideal situation compare to the current situation?

Questions focused on the sale (end of the funnel) sound like:

- How soon are you thinking of making a supplier change?

- What is your budget?

- What criteria will you use to decide on a provider?

- What other options are you considering?

- What do you already know about our company?

This is the proper sequencing of questions for a seller who wants to understand buyer needs and advance the sale toward a proposed solution and, ultimately, to a close.

3. Non-Actionable Questions

Ultimately, a seller's job is to sell. Learning about a buyer's needs is a means to that end. It is a means that serves buyers well and simultaneously helps sellers to be more effective.

But a seller should never lose sight of the fact that he or she is asking quality questions, understanding buyer needs, differentiating, creating value, building trust, strategically planning and aligning with the buyer's process so a sale can be made.

Sellers sometimes do forget that part. They get caught up in the needs assessment process and begin to think of themselves as pro bono consultants to their buyers. The value buyers recognize when sellers ask great questions can be extremely validating. It feels better than hearing "no" and may entice some sellers to camp on the needs assessment phase for prolonged periods of time.

The biggest trap for a seller is pursuing buyer needs that are not actionable. Those needs may be interesting and important. But if the seller

> The biggest trap for a seller is pursuing buyer needs that are not actionable.

cannot offer a solution to a particular need, there must be a reasonable cut-off point to that part of the conversation. That's why sellers should proceed with caution when asking questions about needs they cannot act on.

How far should the seller go? Since the funnel starts out with broad questions about all types of needs, some non-actionable needs are bound to be raised by the buyer. The seller needs to probe those just enough to have context. The seller should not ignore needs expressed by the buyer – the natural flow of conversation shouldn't be disrupted, and the topics discussed do have merit for building trust.

On the other hand, the seller doesn't need to know all the details and dimensions of needs which are unrelated to solutions he or she can offer. This is where using questions to steer the conversation comes into play. The seller, by asking questions true to his or her strategic intent, can redirect without dismissing what the buyer has said.

The first step, then, is to understand the broad need. A seller should listen closely for clues about how he or she can be a part of the solution. Then, after probing the need, the seller must decide if there is a potential link to a solution he or she can provide. If not, then the seller should ask a question to probe another potential need (without moving too hastily to a sales-focused question).

This sales meeting illustrates how a seller manages to direct the conversation to actionable needs without becoming sales focused. Note, too, how naturally the conversation flows even though this restaurant supply seller is continually steering the conversation with her questions. As she works through the funnel of questions, you can also see how she moves away from non-actionable areas.

Seller: Thanks for meeting with me today. What I'm hoping to do first is learn more about your current business needs. Would you mind if I asked you a few questions?

Buyer: No, not at all.

Seller: I see from your website that earnings are up INSIDE THE SALES CALL following the recent announcement about adding eight new restaurants. What's the timeline for the openings?

Buyer: We've got real estate deals on five of the eight, so we'll have those open within six months. The other markets have been a little more challenging due to land use regulations and higher costs in California.

Seller: What will it mean to you when all eight are open?

Buyer: Mainly it will mean my boss stops breathing down my neck. I'm doing all I can, but the pressure's been intense.

Seller: What is your boss concerned about most?

Buyer: We've made a huge commitment. Ever since we went public, the pressure's been more and more intense. When you deliver, you're expected to deliver even more. If you don't deliver, there's no second chance. He's worried about his next promotion, and he's tired of being under the microscope, too.

Seller: How important is it, then, for these five restaurant openings to go smoothly?

Buyer: Well, obviously, we have no room to screw up on those. We need to be on time or even ahead of time because that would cushion some of the fallout if the others lag behind.

Seller: Describe for me what it will take to make those openings as smooth as possible.

Buyer: First and foremost, we can't have any supplier delays. I lost a total of 82 selling days last year on delayed openings when our orders weren't fulfilled on time. That's unacceptable.

Seller: I heard about that at a trade show. I agree those delays should not have happened. You're absolutely right to expect timely order fulfillment. What else would you expect to see from a new supplier?

Buyer: I just want to work with someone who's a straight shooter. I don't have a whole lot of time to waste on back-and-forth negotiations.

Just give me your best price in the first quote, you know? I also don't have time to triple check every detail and explain every order. I need to work with someone who knows what's involved in design, shipping and installation.

Seller: What else will you be considering as you decide on a new supplier?

Buyer: I'll be looking closely at company reputation and client lists. We can't take any chances on reliability. After that, I guess the only other thing we expect is a collaborative partnership. We're going to be one of the largest customers for any supplier we choose, so I expect to have some clout.

Seller: Just to help me understand the scope, what do you typically budget for the full outfitting of each location?

The seller moved from very broad questions to very narrow questions within a 10-minute interview. It doesn't always come about this quickly or flow this smoothly, especially when you first begin using questioning techniques. But for the purposes of illustrating how to avoid non-actionable topics, this is a solid example.

There are three times during this interview when the seller redirected to ensure buyer needs were revealed. The buyer needs the seller could support were the ones discussed most. The seller chose not to ask about California delays. The seller did not invite the buyer to vent about her boss. The seller moved away from complaints about shareholder pressures. She knew she could not provide any actionable solutions for these challenges. By being strategic in the questions she crafted, the seller was very efficient.

The seller focused on what she could potentially solve. She extracted something from every buyer statement and used what she heard as building blocks. She steered the conversation with the follow-up questions she asked. Every question was deliberate and purposeful. Her intention was to peel back the need and understand it more fully without becoming enmeshed in needs she couldn't address.

The buyer was impressed with the seller and felt she was professional, knowledgeable and collaborative. The seller learned exactly what she needed to know in order to provide a solution laden with buyer benefits that were relevant, meaningful and highly customized to this particular buyer at this exact point in time.

4. Scripted Questions

There is one last precaution for asking questions. For sellers who are new to asking questions, it is tempting to rely on pre-scripted questions. After all, there are many resources for effective sales questions and planning ahead could eliminate some of the challenges related to asking the "wrong" questions and/or constructing less effective questions.

But scripted questions should be avoided. They aren't natural, and they will interfere with the seller's ability to stay in the moment and conduct an interchange of ideas and information. Scripting questions before a buyer meeting causes

> **Avoiding the wrong questions leaves room for the right ones.**

sellers to depend on what's written and miss opportunities to ask follow-up questions stemming from natural curiosity. Scripted questions feel impersonal and manipulative to buyers.

The other significant risk of relying on scripted questions is the implication needs assessment is a one-time event. But sellers who are operating with a strategic plan to understand buyer needs will be prepared to ask questions at any time, as buyer needs change frequently and unexpectedly.

Sellers who master the skills of question-asking won't need to depend on scripted questions. Instead, they will be fully equipped at any time to steer conversations with buyers so they can readily identify actionable needs, avoid asking manipulative questions, properly sequence questions to drill down from broad buyer needs to narrower needs linked to their own products, and advance sales smoothly.

Avoiding the wrong questions leaves room for the right ones.

CHAPTER 11
Listening for Content & Feeling

This section on asking strategic questions wouldn't be complete without also covering what to do after a quality question has been asked.

Like so many of the skills discussed in this book, the skill of listening seems basic. It may seem as if no attention to it should be needed. But the widely held perception that listening is elementary is exactly why it requires our attention here.

In school and in most sales training courses, we are not taught how to ask questions or how to listen. These are critical skills distinguishing a top seller from an average one. Empowered buyers are demanding to be heard **and** to be challenged with new ideas **and** to have unique value created for them by sellers. None of this is possible without solid questioning skills and sharp listening skills.

In school speech classes and in business conversations, the emphasis is on eloquent speaking skills. Middle school communication classes are packed with assignments related to preparing and giving speeches. In a way, these classes inadvertently teach students how to stop listening. While one student uncomfortably presents, all the other students are expected to sit quietly and wait for their turns. Listening isn't part of the program. As adults, we participate in business meetings where conversations become competitions to see who can speak the loudest, say the most, dominate the conversation and make their point stick.

On top of that, there are workplace expectations and societal norms placing a high value on multi-tasking. Most of our listening is done while we are driving, checking our e-mail, killing time while commercials air, and so on. At a minimum, we listen at the same time we are planning our responses to what's being said. This practice of partial listening is widespread. The next time you go grocery shopping, observe how many people are talking on cell phones while they shop. It's no small number. All this activity that accompanies listening takes its toll. We don't have the habits or skills of active listening sellers truly need.

The loss is not quantifiable so it's easy to overlook. But few would disagree there certainly is a loss when we don't fully listen to others. You notice it in your own day-to-day conversations. No matter how commonplace it may be, it

> **There certainly is a loss when we don't fully listen to others.**

doesn't feel good when we know we've only been partially heard because others were distracted. For a buyer, being asked to trust a seller who doesn't listen well is particularly distasteful. Sellers who actively listen have yet another opportunity to differentiate themselves since so few do this.

This term, active listening, refers to a higher standard of listening. First, there's hearing. That's a passive function, one that requires no effort at all for most. Listening is hearing plus paying attention to take in what's being said. Active listening goes beyond listening to include paying close attention, focusing to eliminate distractions and devoting mental effort to process what's being said. Active listening isn't easy and doesn't come naturally.

When people are actively listening, they respond differently than those who are only partly engaged. Active listeners:

- Don't interrupt.

- Don't respond hastily, as soon as an opening becomes available.

- Don't play a "one up" game to try and match each point made.

- Don't jump to conclusions.

- Don't judge what is being said too quickly.

- Don't interject with an unsolicited or premature solution.

Instead, active listeners:

- Probe for clarification, back story, details and feelings.

- Listen for both content and feeling.

- Empathize by putting themselves in the speaker's shoes.

- Listen for what's different, not just for what's familiar.

- Take what's being said seriously.

- Spot their own assumptions or biases about what's being said.

- Eliminate distractions while listening so they can focus fully.

- Hear the whole story before judging or responding.

- Encourage the speaker with attention and body language.

- Look at the speaker or, perhaps, take notes on what's being said.

- Never seem rushed, bored or impatient.

Developing Your Active Listening Skills

Developing active listening skills is as easy as (and as difficult as) developing a new habit. A seller has to commit to changing what he or she is doing while listening.

The easiest way to start developing new habits for active listening is by taking inventory of your current listening habits. When someone else is talking, make note of your own behaviors. Catch

> A seller has to commit to changing what he or she is doing while listening.

yourself when your mind wanders and re-center your attention on the speaker. You will have to do this even when you begin mentally weighing your options for how to respond. If you do, your response will be better because you won't miss what the speaker says next.

One tip for focusing your listening is to jot down any disruptive thoughts. Writing them down will assure you can come back to those thoughts, and you'll release the mental energy it takes to hang on to them.

Another tip to focus your listening and prevent you from interrupting or playing a "one up" game is to listen for what is unfamiliar instead of for what's familiar. Our brains naturally tune in to what is familiar to us but, by doing so,

> **Deliberately practice listening for what is different.**

we can easily miss what's new or different. When you deliberately practice listening for what is different – unfamiliar, new, unusual, unlike what you've seen or heard before – you will find your mental processing takes more time and keeps you focused longer and better.

These two tips are starting points for forming better listening habits. If a seller starts with just these two tips and works to improve his or her active listening skills, there will be a distinct differentiation as compared to other sellers. This, coupled with a strategic intent to fully understand customer needs, will give you a clear advantage.

What to Do With the Information You Gather

Armed with quality questions and superior listening skills, a seller can expect to build trust and create value for buyers. But there's one more critical aspect to bring this all together in order to deliver solid solutions for buyers. Sellers need to know what to do with the information they gather. They need to know how to ask questions, how to listen, and what to do with what they've learned.

When a seller fumbles between uncovering a buyer need and crafting a solution to meet the need, the problem usually has one of two causes. The first cause is related to poor listening and the second is related to not being able to think from the buyer's perspective (which can often be resolved by listening to understand the buyer). Both problems can be solved by fine tuning your listening skills.

Poor listening is evident when a seller offers a solution that doesn't quite match what the buyer stated as a need. In role play exercises used during sales training programs, it is not uncommon for a group of 12-15 sellers to hear the same buyer need but then play it back so it seems there were 10 or more different needs.

Why the discrepancies?

Sometimes, it's because sellers hear something similar to what they've heard before or similar to what they hope to hear. They make assumptions that add to or take away from what a unique buyer has said in this time and place. For example, an advertising seller calling on a franchise financial planner heard the need "I'd like to be number one" instead of the exact words "I'm hoping to be the top seller in the region." The reason this mattered is the seller proposed a national online campaign, something

INSIDE THE SALES CALL

the buyer was prohibited from running due to corporate practices protecting other franchisees from encroachment.

Missing the words "in the region" made a big difference. The seller missed them because he wanted to sell a national online campaign, and he selectively filtered out the information that didn't fit – not intentionally, but sub-consciously. He knew what he'd done as soon as the buyer corrected him. He acknowledged having a nagging reservation in the back of his mind even as he was preparing the proposal, but he was driven by the desire to sell what was in the forefront for him. Selective hearing and the self-serving solutions resulting from it impair connections with buyers.

Sometimes, the solution offered isn't a match to the buyer's needs because the seller limits the scope. The buyer may be thinking bigger, but the

> **Buyers are time-pressed and demand responsiveness.**

seller is accustomed to hearing "no" or to making smaller sales. The buyer says "Component parts are a good start, but I'd like to make a complete shift to streamline all our purchasing." The seller returns with a proposal for a fraction of the component parts. Why? Because, according to the seller, it would be easier to get the smaller sale first, and she wasn't sure the buyer was serious about making a complete shift.

Delivering a solution with less than the buyer needs is no better than offering something he doesn't need at all. Buyers are time-pressed and demand responsiveness. A seller's lack of confidence isn't likely to inspire buyer confidence. More to the point, though, when a buyer says exactly what he needs or wants, the seller must respond in full. To do so, a savvy seller first listens, checking for understanding to overcome self-imposed limitations and anything else that obfuscates the buyer's stated needs.

The third reason sellers miss the mark on creating solutions linked directly to buyer needs is they don't have clarity on which need to meet. If the buyer describes multiple needs, the seller should then ask follow-up questions to understand which need is most urgent or

> **The seller who delivers on what matters most to the buyer is the one who will earn the business.**

pressing. This is always related to what the buyer's current hierarchy of value is, and a seller should not presume to know what's most or least important.

When the seller picks which need(s) to meet, he could leave the buyer's larger needs unmet. That opens the door to competitors who will seize the opportunity to deliver what you did not. Sellers who go for the easy sale (fastest, cheapest, most popular) are often left wondering why the buyer chose something more expensive or completely different from a competitor. It always boils down to this: the seller who delivers on what matters most to the buyer is the one who will earn the business.

To understand what matters most, sellers have to ask questions and then listen for content and feeling. With DISCOVER Questions®, described in the next section of this book, sellers will be prepared to ask questions that pinpoint what each buyer values most. When the buyer responds to these questions, a seller will have a better understanding of the buyer's priorities and the buyer's hierarchy of value.

Listening for Feeling

In addition to the information shared in a direct response, sellers are also advised to listen for feeling. The content of an answer refers to the words that are spoken. In addition to those words, the seller should be listening and observing for clues about feelings. This is especially true when potentially sensitive questions are asked.

Consider this situation. A buyer shared her needs for faster turnaround on production, overnight delivery and custom design work. She also wanted to see a reduction in the cost per unit. The seller didn't think it was possible to meet all these needs since the increases in production and shipping costs would be prohibitive when it came to negotiating for a volume discount. So the seller asked the buyer "Of all these needs you've described, which one is the most important to you?" The buyer

INSIDE THE SALES CALL

replied "Oh, I suppose if I had to pick then I'd have to go with the cost reduction."

If listening to content alone, the seller would have brought back a proposal to meet the need for a lower cost per unit. But this seller listened for feeling, too, and noticed the disappointment expressed when the buyer contemplated giving up the other needs. So the seller followed up to ask "It sounds like you have to say cost but wish you could choose something else. If you could, what would it be?"

The buyer immediately expressed gratitude for the seller picking up on this cue. She perked up and showed a great deal of enthusiasm for the custom design work which, it turned out, had been developed by her daughter in a contest during the company's take-your-child-to-work-day activities. Since the custom design work was the least costly of the desired changes, the seller was able to deliver on both needs – the one the company demanded and the one the buyer was emotionally invested in, too.

As with asking quality questions, developing and using active listening skills will be easier for sellers who are mindful of and dedicated to the strategic intent of fully understanding buyer needs. Advancing the sale requires staying aligned with buyers. Actively listening to buyers maximizes your alignment. This is how you will become the one seller buyers WANT to talk to.

PART II
USING DISCOVER QUESTIONS® TO CONNECT

In the movie Spiderman, Uncle Ben tells Peter Parker "With great power comes great responsibility." This section on introducing DISCOVER Questions® will give you incredible power to connect with your buyers. To learn more about the great responsibility you bear in using these questions and wielding your newfound power, refer back to Part I. The tiebacks are also flagged for you here in Part II.

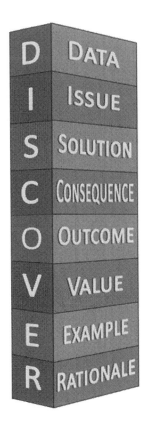

CHAPTER 12
Introduction to DISCOVER Questions®

In Part I of this book, we reviewed important reminders about why asking questions is so important for a professional seller as well as how to craft compelling questions to create value for your buyers. Those first 11 chapters are a refresher for the serious student of sales.

Before launching directly into what is new and unique in this book, it was important to review the fundamentals. Strengthening your skills in the basics will make you far more effective in applying this research and the DISCOVER Questions® methodology. For those who are starting here, jumping right into DISCOVER Questions®, I've included tiebacks to previous chapters you can use as needed.

In the next eight chapters, we will examine eight different kinds of questions. Each is represented by a letter in the apt and easy-to-remember acronym D-I-S-C-O-V-E-R. Each type of question has a specific purpose. Learning about and using all eight types of questions will prepare sellers to masterfully steer sales conversations and rapidly gather information. When all eight types of questions are included in a conversation, buyers' perceptions of sellers are dramatically improved. These questions solidify relationships by creating value for the individual buyer, differentiating sellers from their competitors and building trust.

> **There is no magic in any one question.**

Please note this is not a set of scripted questions. There is no magic in any one question or in any pre-determined combination of questions. While plenty of questions are included here as examples of each type, this is by no means a complete list of all possible questions. Sellers are strongly encouraged to learn about the purpose for each type of question and then to craft their own questions of each type. That doesn't mean creating a single set of questions to be used over and over again. It means staying in the moment, letting curiosity be your guide, letting the conversation flow naturally and steering it with appropriately placed DISCOVER Questions® you craft on the spot to suit the situation and advance the sale.

The magic of DISCOVER Questions® comes in mastering the process of thinking strategically before you ask a question. When you develop an understanding of the eight different purposes for asking questions, the agility to phrase your questions so they yield exactly the type of information you are seeking, and the discipline of sticking to your pre-determined intent for asking questions, you will be amazed by how much information you can gather in a short period of time. Like many sellers who use DISCOVER Questions® and the techniques described in Part I of this book, you will be the one seller in your industry customers actively seek out, the one prospects happily call back. You will stand out because you will connect with buyers and create value for them every time you meet.

> **The magic of DISCOVER Questions® comes in mastering the process of thinking strategically before you ask a question.**

These bold claims are backed up by sales professionals in many industries, selling to all sorts of buyers, entering in with varied levels of experience, working with a wide range of budgets, and with only one thing in common – a desire to increase their sales by more effectively meeting the needs of buyers.

These claims are also backed up by the people who did business with these sellers. Buyers' reactions to DISCOVER Questions® are very revealing. You'll notice an immediate improvement in how buyers respond to you, too, when you implement these techniques and know the purpose of your questions. You can expect higher levels of engagement, more returned calls and more satisfied customers. In the next eight chapters, we'll include what buyers say about each one of the question types so you can see the full picture – the purpose of the question type, when and how to use it, and how buyers feel about it.

How DISCOVER Questions® Were Developed

First, let's backtrack to explain how and why DISCOVER Questions® were researched and developed. It all started with my own interest in research done by the Huthwaite Institute and the resulting methodology known as S.P.I.N. Selling. For me, a high-achieving sales rep at the time, the research and methodology were fascinating. Here was a common sense, easy-to-follow way to engage buyers! I used this approach and became a true believer.

At the same time, I also felt constrained. There were only four narrow types of questions used in S.P.I.N., which left a whole lot of valid questions that didn't quite fit the model. Additionally, for me, the questions prescribed sometimes became robotic and a bit worn out. You can only ask the same set of questions to the same customer a few times before you need more to work with. Don't misunderstand – S.P.I.N. Selling is highly effective with certain types of accounts and in certain situations. For the work I was doing, I just needed something more. I needed to dive deeper with my accounts.

So I conducted my own research. Initially, as a sales manager, I accompanied sales reps in 14 territories on sales calls. I took copious notes about the questions they asked. Later, as a sales trainer and field coach, I had opportunities to ride along on sales calls with nearly 100 sales reps.

Eventually, I moved into a corporate role with a Fortune 500 company. There, a team of 22 sales trainers and field coaches worked with me and continued this research, writing down questions asked and how buyers responded. Working as a charter member of the Sales Force Advisory Board, I also worked internationally with senior sales leaders across many industries to understand how questions were being used in selling.

By this point, I'd amassed reams of research about questions. I was convinced there were more than four narrow types of questions used in selling, so I began bucketing all these questions collected in the field and in training role plays. I concluded there were eight types. In the seven years since, I've been on the lookout for outliers. Although my field research has continued, I haven't yet heard a single question that doesn't fit neatly into one of these eight types.

DISCOVER Questions®

Illustration 6

The word DISCOVER is a fitting acronym for these eight types of questions. You see, what makes one type of question different from another is its purpose. There are eight distinct reasons to ask questions. Used collectively, the central purpose of asking a variety of quality questions has this result: the person doing the asking will discover a great deal about the person who is answering questions.

Like the questions themselves, the process of discovery is powerful. Discover means "to see, get knowledge of, learn, find, or understand something new." In sales, to discover means to expand what you know about your buyer so you can expand what you can do for your buyer. That's the true magic of DISCOVER Questions®.

Thinking about the purpose of a question before you ask it takes a little getting used to before it comes naturally. Generally, we ask questions because we want to know something. Oftentimes, we haven't quite figured out what we want to know before we ask the question. Therefore, our initial question is a vague placeholder to buy a little time for thinking about the real question we want to ask next. Additionally, we may not

> **Without forethought, there is indeed a risk that a question won't be productive.**

pause to consider the way a question will be received. We simultaneously form and speak the question.

This is why asking questions feels risky. Without forethought, there is indeed a risk that a question won't be productive. It may even cause a negative reaction if we are too quick, too casual or too cavalier with our questions.

It's easier to know and plan around just eight types of questions. When you can start out by thinking "which of these purposes do I have for the question I'm about to ask?" then you will ask questions that are more articulate and more specific in the way they are phrased. You will be clear on what you are looking for, and your clarity will be apparent to your buyers. They will give you, in response to your questions, exactly what you wanted to know.

When asking questions, you have a certain obligation to manage the conversation. You do this by thoughtfully constructing purposeful questions. Here are a few examples to illustrate the difference between a vague question and one that is clear and purposeful.

Vague: How are sales these days?

Clear: What is your adjusted sales goal for the third quarter?

Purpose: To pinpoint the target or outcome this buyer is aiming for.

INSIDE THE SALES CALL

Vague: What's new?

Clear: What progress are you making on your data project?

Purpose: To get a specific update on a project related to the seller's field.

Vague: Tell me about the concerns you have.

Clear: What is your number one concern about making a move?

Purpose: To understand the most critical reservation and its priority.

No More Fishing Expeditions

When a seller asks purposeful questions, he will avoid the perception he is conducting a "fishing expedition" that is unproductive and time-consuming. He will engage buyers rather than causing them to feel threatened by poorly worded questions or suspicious of aimless ones.

With only eight types of questions representing eight broad purposes for asking questions, sellers can easily learn and use DISCOVER Questions® in order to better understand and address their buyers' needs. Typically, sellers use two or three of these question types most frequently, so adding new types of questions expands the breadth of information yielded from the buyer.

The eight purposes of asking questions are:

- To gather facts. These are **D**ata Questions.

- To probe or avoid problems in a relationship. These are **I**ssue Questions.

- To introduce alternatives or new ideas. These are **S**olution Questions.

- To call attention to potential risks, concerns or challenges. These are **C**onsequence Questions.

- To learn about desired outcomes. These are **O**utcome Questions.

- To prioritize and clarify what's most important. These are **V**alue Questions.

- To create a concrete example or contrast. These are **E**xample Questions

- To understand how a decision has been or will be made. These are **R**ationale Questions.

Every question you ask has, at its core, one of these eight purposes. At this time, you may not deliberately consider the purpose before verbalizing your question. In fact, when asked "why did you ask that particular question?" most sellers are unable to immediately explain their reasons. But given time to think through what they really intended, there is always a link back to one of these eight purposes.

> **There is always a link back to one of these eight purposes.**

This is true outside of sales, too. DISCOVER Questions® have also been observed, field-tested, trained and researched with non-selling groups including managers, leaders, trainers and coaches. People who learn about on-the-job applications for these purposeful questions report heightened awareness and a strategic use of questions carrying over into their personal lives, too.

The Most Commonly Used Types

Of these eight types of questions, three types are more familiar, more comfortable and more commonly used. In field research, these are the three sellers use to start needs assessment interviews and the three asked most frequently. In training role plays, these same three show up as "safety net" questions. When sellers are feeling uncomfortable or uncertain about where to go next in a role play, they consistently revert back to these three types.

You can track this for yourself. As you begin working with DISCOVER Questions®., monitor the types of questions you naturally ask in selling and in non-selling conversations. Your awareness that there are other types of questions with their own discrete purposes will help you later to integrate those additional types of questions when needed.

The three most commonly used types of questions are the ones with these purposes:

- To gather facts (**D**ata Questions).

- To probe or avoid problems in a relationship (**I**ssue Questions).

- To learn about desired outcomes (**O**utcome Questions).

From the buyer's point of view, these can be perceived as "throwaway" questions because they don't create as much value as the other five types of questions. Sellers who put too much stock in these three types limit the value they create for their buyers. These questions are also the most superficial and the most overused. If every seller is asking these types of questions, it's no wonder buyers see little value in time spent answering them.

Questions used for the purpose of gathering facts (**D**ata Questions) create little value for the buyer because the buyer already knows the answers. These questions are not thought-provoking or interesting.

Questions used for the purpose of probing or avoiding problems in a relationship (**I**ssue Questions) can seem insincere or self-serving if they are not used judiciously. The question "how are you today?" is a good example.

When sellers ask this de rigueur question without genuine interest in the response, it defeats the purpose of the question. Similarly, questions asked in response to a buyer's complaint won't preserve the relationship if the questions the seller asks about the problem seem to be defensive.

Questions used for the purpose of learning about the buyer's desired outcomes (Outcome Questions) seem to be the easiest ones for sellers to ask. Initially, buyers rather like these questions, too. Unfortunately, these questions can backfire if a seller is hasty in moving straight into a sales pitch just as soon as the buyer offers even the slightest hint of a desired outcome.

> **The purposes of these most commonly asked questions can get lost in the seller's application of them.**

In short, the purposes of these most commonly asked question can get lost in the seller's application of them. That's why we will also devote a chapter to these three question types, shoring up your understanding of their purposes and offering some alternative ways to phrase these questions and follow up on them so they create value for buyers.

As you improve your facility with all eight types of DISCOVER Questions®, you will apply them in all sorts of selling situations. Each type of question is highly valuable in needs assessment and negotiation. Some questions are useful in opening the sale and getting past gatekeepers while others are effective in trial closing and closing the sale. Working to understand the purpose of each question type and how it is perceived by buyers will help you determine the right timing for each type of question in each unique situation.

Combining an understanding of question purpose with your buyer-based intentions and well-constructed, open-ended questions will enable you to advance the sale more quickly and more often.

CHAPTER 13
Data Questions

The D in DISCOVER Questions® stands for Data Questions. The purpose of these questions is to gather facts.

Data Questions solicit information that is provable, factual and objective. There are no subjective opinions involved when asking Data Questions. The information provided will always be historical or, perhaps, current. But there are no Data Questions about the future because the future state cannot be proven.

> **Do your fact-gathering ahead of a sales call rather than during the sales call.**

Sellers should use Data Questions sparingly. It is best to do your fact-gathering ahead of a sales call rather than during the sales call. You can research your prospects and customers online and in trade publications. This will save your buyers time and will prevent you from asking too many low value Data Questions.

The reason Data Questions are low value for the buyer is the buyer already knows the answers or can readily access the information. There is no thought required and no stimulation of new ideas. These questions are not the type that will generate expansive answers from the buyer nor yield deep insights for the seller.

Additionally, Data Questions do not build trust or rapport the way other question types will. When used in moderation, Data Questions are viewed neutrally by buyers. In some cases, however, they may cause a buyer to wonder what a seller will do with the information provided. That's why it's important to signal your intent to the buyer before asking these questions (see chapter 7).

Buyers respond negatively to Data Questions when they feel the intelligence gathering is premature in asking about sensitive matters or confidential information. There is only so much information needed to make a sales recommendation. Until there is a green light for moving forward with detailed specifications, smart sellers will selectively limit Data Questions to get the basics.

Likewise, buyers may not appreciate Data Questions at times when they are feeling protective of their information. That's why it is best to plan way ahead for negotiations, routinely gathering information in each meeting with a buyer rather than trying to get it all at once. The time when you want it most is the time when it's least likely to be shared, so ask questions early and often!

Despite these "use with care" considerations, sellers will need Data Questions when they are purposefully gathering factual information. As with all question types, Data Questions should be open-ended and clearly worded so they are not vague or confusing.

Examples of Data Questions

These are examples of Data Questions commonly used in selling. Remember, this list is not provided as a "cut and paste" set of questions for you to use with your buyers. Asking any question without clearly understanding what information you would like to obtain (and how you will use it) will make you less effective and less credible with your buyers. Instead, use this list to get a fuller understanding about what Data Questions are and to prompt your own thinking about Data Questions you can use with your buyers.

- What are you currently paying for shipping?

- When was your business established?

- Who have you purchased from in the past?

- On an annualized basis, what volume have you been moving?

- Where are your distribution centers located?

- What percentages of your total sales are generated by each region?

- How many new users did you add last year?

- What is the stated Mission of the company?

- Over the past five years, which has been your best-selling item?

- What is the total square footage?

Notice there are no Data Questions with a future tense. What will happen in the future is not provable or certain, so Data Questions are not used to ask about the future.

There is a difference between asking "What is the forecast growth rate in your annual plan?" and "What do you hope to achieve this year?" The first question is a Data Question because it asks for something in the past – what was forecast. What **was** forecast will not change even if the forecast is revised. The information captured in the annual plan is a constant, even if the eventual outcomes vary from the plan.

The first question, unlike the second, does not ask about a subjective hope. It does not ask about something that could change. The first question, then, is a Data Question. The second one is not. (It's an Outcome Question… more about those can be found in Chapter 17.)

Notice, too, none of these bulleted sample questions asks for an opinion.

Facts are the opposite of opinions. Fact-based questions have only one correct answer while opinion-based questions could be answered differently by every person you ask. Keep facts and opinions delineated by posing your questions carefully and clearly. When a seller prefaces a Data Question by saying "What do you think?" or "I'd like to get your opinion," then the purpose of the question is no longer clear. The seller may not know if the buyer's response is fact-based or opinion-based.

Having a clear purpose in mind before delivering the question is imperative. If you want facts, ask a question like the ones shown in this chapter. If you are looking instead for an opinion, you'll find other question types to be more useful for meeting your purpose.

Balancing Data Questions

The purpose of asking Data Questions is to gather factual information. If a seller is clear in stating the intent for asking these questions, buyers will be more tolerant and patient while these questions are being asked. Better yet, if a seller mixes in other types of DISCOVER Questions®, buyers will scarcely notice when a fact-based question is asked and answered. That's the ideal situation.

What prevents sellers from conducting needs assessments with a variety of question types is usually their own lack of awareness about other types of questions and their own misunderstanding about the purpose and value of other question types. When sellers stick exclusively to or primarily to Data Questions they miss opportunities to create value.

If you are initially skeptical about using other types of questions, try this. Open your needs assessment with two Data Questions. Being comfortable with these starter questions will give you confidence at the beginning of the meeting. Observe the way your buyer responds to these questions, in a matter-of-fact manner and with brief answers.

Make your third question a different type of question. Use something you learned in response to the first two questions and probe to elicit an opinion or future-focused perspective. You could even make your third question a little more personal, specific to the buyer rather than to his or her company. Watch what happens. You will get a rich response with a wealth of information to consider later as you prepare a solution. It's important to see for yourself how buyers respond to a variety of question types. Once you do, you will recognize the value in expanding your range of question types.

Consider the difference between these two interviews, one focusing exclusively on facts and figures and the other using a mix of question types. For your initial read through, don't worry about understanding each of the question types – you'll get caught up on that as you read the next seven chapters of this book. Do, however, note how many Data Questions appear in each interview and what the impact is of mixing up question types.

Interview #1, heavily focused on facts:

Seller: How long have you been in business? *Data Question*

Buyer: Nearly 22 years.

Seller: Always at this location? *Data Question*

Buyer: Yep.

Seller: What are your average annual sales? *Data Question*

Buyer: Last year was just under $460,000. Pretty typical for a full service single location restaurant.

Seller: On a weekend night, how many table turnovers do you get at dinner? *Data Question*

INSIDE THE SALES CALL

Buyer: Between two and three, depending on time of year. People stay longer in the summer and during holiday season.

Seller: How many employees do you have on staff? *Data Question*

Buyer: We're a little lean right now with 11 people. I'll hire up to 14 for weekends in the summer.

Using five Data Questions, the seller learned several facts about this business. The buyer was able to answer each question without delay as these are standard metrics tracked by most restaurants. What's lacking in this interview, however, is a natural conversational flow. It sounds more like a survey than a dialogue.

Interview #2, mixing question types to elicit opinions and generate ideas

Seller: I see you've been in business here for over 21 years. A lot has changed for restaurants over that time period. What's been most challenging for you? *Consequence Question*

Buyer: We've had our fair share of challenges over the years. It's tougher now than ever before because ╎INSIDE THE SALES CALL╎ the cost of everything is increasing – minimum wage got voted up, wholesale food prices and transportation costs are up, printing costs and website maintenance plus utilities... You name it and I'm paying more for it than I did last year.

Seller: What workarounds or adjustments are you making in order to maintain profitability? *Solution Question*

Buyer: I'm running a little low on staffing, working a few more hours myself. We're also cutting back on portion sizes which works out good because diners are looking for healthier plates. It also gets people in and out a little quicker so we can turn tables.

Seller: With these changes in place, what are your annual sales and profit margin projected to be this year? *Outcome Question*

Buyer: We're showing a 2.6% uptick in sales which will put us at about $471,000 in total sales by year end if it continues. That will be our best year in revenue. But profit is a different story. I'm struggling to hold steady at 2% and may have to raise menu prices to make it this year.

Seller: How important is it to stay at 2% or better? *Value Question*

Buyer: It's absolutely critical. See, we've got a 2-year expansion plan to open a same name bistro in Midtown. We can't get bank financing if we are losing ground at this location.

Seller: What is it about Midtown that caused you to consider opening a bistro format there? *Rationale Question*

Buyer: It's where the growth is with all those lofts and condos attracting people who used to be out here. Our familiar name isn't enough to draw them out of the city. But it would pull 'em in if we were right there where they are.

Same number of questions, five in total. But the seller in the second interview asked five different types of questions and followed the natural course of conversation. There were no Data Questions, but the facts offered in the buyer's responses provided ample information for the seller. People often provide facts to give us context whether we ask for facts or not.

The value of the questions asked in the second interview is apparent. For the seller, there is significantly more to work with in preparing a relevant and compelling proposal. For the buyer, there is a comfort level with the seller as a result of the empathy and understanding expressed in asking questions demonstrating both knowledge of the industry and an interest in the unique buyer.

If you were the buyer, which one of these two sellers would you trust more? Which would you feel had engaged you and had more to offer? Which would you book a second sales appointment with for a proposal presentation?

People don't care how much you know until they know how much you care. Exclusively asking Data Questions makes it very difficult to convey you care and are able to create value. They are essential questions, but they are not meant to stand alone.

Use Data Questions to gather facts from the buyer when there is no other resource available to provide factual information. Then branch out to build on the key facts by asking the other seven types of DISCOVER Questions®. To learn how, just keep reading!

CHAPTER 14
Issue Questions

The I in DISCOVER Questions® stands for Issue Questions. The purpose of these questions is to probe or avoid problems in a relationship.

All Issue Questions pertain to the relationship between the buyer and the seller (or their respective companies). This is the only type of question intended to be about the seller. The other seven types of questions are intended to focus on the buyer.

There are two situations that call for Issue Questions. The first is in response to a concern or problem the buyer has raised, an issue requiring attention in order to maintain or enhance the relationship. The second way to use an Issue Question is in a proactive mode, with the seller checking in with the buyer to avoid any future issues.

Issue Questions are commonly asked by sellers, but they are not asked effectively. Sellers also respond ineffectively when buyers answer Issue Questions. You can differentiate yourself from competitors if you ask Issue Questions without getting defensive about buyers' responses. Buyers respond

> **It's better to know upfront when a problem is brewing.**

favorably to these questions in both the reactive and the proactive scenarios as long as the seller is genuinely open to their responses. But some sellers think just the opposite, that buyers will respond negatively if invited to express their concerns.

Even if a buyer does respond negatively to an Issue Question, it's still in your best interest to ask it. Any time a buyer harbors negative feelings about you, the product you sell or your company, there is an opening for a competitor to steal away the buyer's business. It's better to know upfront when a problem is brewing or there is some dissatisfaction to be dealt with instead of being blindsided when you lose the business and don't know why.

Besides, Issue Questions don't cause issues. They merely open the discussion about an existing issue or invite more information so problems can be resolved.

Reactive Issue Questions

When you ask an Issue Question in response to a buyer's complaint, you can expect two things to happen. First, the buyer will be surprised. Most sellers respond to complaints swiftly with promises and platitudes rather than fully hearing out the buyer. Or they respond defensively to deflect blame. Because you're asking with genuine interest to hear more about the issue, the buyer will be disarmed and less likely to be aggressive or angry in lodging the complaint. People choose those behaviors when they don't feel they are being heard.

> **You are making an investment in the relationship by asking these questions.**

When you respond to a complaint by asking an Issue Question, the second reaction to anticipate is your invitation will be accepted. The buyer will use this opportunity to express any pent-up frustration and to vent. You will have decreased the emotional charge and increased the flow of information.

Since the purpose of Issue Questions is to probe or avoid problems in a relationship, you are making an investment in the relationship by asking these questions. You are signaling how you care enough about the relationship to take a little heat and to understand what caused the dissatisfaction.

Don't confuse being open to hearing a complaint with conflict. You're not inviting conflict. Issue Questions are powerful for averting conflict, defusing the issue before it reaches that level. Issue Questions minimize the problem. They do not create it or maximize it.

Consider these examples of Issue Questions used to probe a problem in a relationship between a buyer and a seller.

- Please tell me more about the error.

- I'd like to understand this fully. Walk me through what happened.

- What do you feel should have been done differently?

- What needs to happen to make this right?

- Your concerns are important to me so please don't hold back. Tell me what's on your mind.

As a buyer, imagine how you'd feel if someone asked you one of these questions when you lodged a complaint. The permission to speak freely and the opportunity to be heard would be a relief. You'd respect and trust the person who responded this way. You would feel secure in the relationship, and you'd be motivated to resolve the issue you'd raised. As a seller, you can make your buyers feel this way, too!

When interviewed about Issue Questions sellers had asked them, buyers reported that they appreciated the question and felt they'd been heard, validated and taken seriously.

Proactive Issue Questions

You don't need to wait for a problem to arise before you make your customers feel they've been heard, validated and taken seriously. Issue Questions can also be used proactively.

135

A proactive Issue Question still serves the purpose of probing or avoiding problems in a relationship. While the reactive use of this type of question is used to probe an existing problem, the proactive use of an Issue Question will help you troubleshoot to avoid problems before they occur.

Buyers respond favorably to the proactive use of Issue Questions, reporting that these also make them feel validated and taken seriously.

A proactive Issue Question can be used as a service check to gauge how the buyer is feeling about the current relationship and interactions with the seller. Here are some examples of proactive Issue Questions.

- What could I be doing differently to make things easier for you?

- I'd like to ask you for an evaluation of my performance as your sales rep. In your opinion, what is working and what is not working?

- Considering other sellers you've worked with, what is something they've done that you wish I would do for you, too?

- What would make our transactions and meetings run more smoothly for you?

- When it comes to working with sellers, what are your biggest pet peeves?

Sure, it takes a little courage to ask these kinds of questions. You don't know what you might hear, and constructive feedback isn't something we are accustomed to inviting. That's why these questions are powerful and differentiating. They set you apart because they demonstrate you care enough about this relationship to be vulnerable and to strive for improvement in your own actions.

Getting your buyer's response to questions like these is far better than the alternative. If you don't know how they are feeling about doing business with you, you are actually in a much more vulnerable state than you will be by asking. Instead of risking a little sting of emotion when you hear the feedback, you're taking the greater risk of potentially continuing to do something irritating or offensive to the buyer. That risk leaves you open to a competitor who can steal your customer.

> **It takes a little courage to ask these kinds of questions.**

Responding to Buyer's Feedback

When you ask Issue Questions, be mindful that you are setting expectations, too. Listening to the buyer's feedback and allowing the buyer to vent is only the first step. By asking and listening, you are implying a promise of change. You are indicating your willingness to try and do something different.

In relationships, listening and understanding count for a lot more than we think. The action you take to listen and understand is every bit as important as your next steps will be. If what the buyer is asking you to do is something you cannot do, you need to say so. It's perfectly okay to set reasonable expectations. There will never be a better time to do so than at this moment when you've carefully listened and probed to understand.

Acknowledging your limitations doesn't undo the favorable impression you've made by inviting the buyer to share an issue with you. There is no requirement for you to acquiesce on every request the buyer makes simply because you invited the feedback. It's the listening and understanding that count.

By the same token, you should try to work with the customer's requests whenever possible. Say "no" to what you cannot do and "yes" to what you

can do. Be clear in defining what you will
and will not do going forward so there are
no misunderstandings. You've built trust
by asking Issue Questions. Now you need

> **Your customer's feedback is a gift to you. Receive it graciously.**

to build on it by maintaining credibility in your follow through.

One last word of caution with Issue Questions: don't respond defensively to what you hear. Your customer's feedback is a gift to you. Receive it graciously. There is no need to assign the blame to others inside your organization. There is no benefit in deflecting the criticism or justifying errors with excuses. There is no upside to counter-attacking out of an emotional response.

Instead of being defensive, be grateful. Thank your customer for sharing this information with you and giving you a chance to rectify the situation. Take this opportunity to learn something new about yourself, your product or your company. After all, you truly do appreciate this feedback being shared with you because the likelihood of retaining this business has increased just by virtue of the conversation you initiated with your Issue Question.

Like the other seven types of DISCOVER Questions®, Issue Questions help sellers connect with buyers. Turn back to Chapter 2 if you are unclear about ways to show your buyer how much you care. You can add asking Issue Questions to the list of ways you can align your selling with what's of value to your buyer.

CHAPTER 15
Solutions Questions

The S in DISCOVER Questions® stands for Solution Questions. The purpose of these questions is to introduce alternatives or new ideas.

Solution Questions plant seeds for ideas you may wish to present in the proposal phase of your sales process. They gauge the buyer's initial reaction so you will be equipped later to handle potential objections. They also promote brainstorming and the generation of new ideas, making these questions high value for the buyer.

Solution Questions can also be used when you want the buyer to self-discover or recall alternatives to what they are currently doing or buying. As a seller, you don't have to have all the answers. You can create value by drawing out what's in the deep recesses of your buyer's mind.

Rather than freewheeling with your unsolicited and untested ideas, you can involve your buyer in generating, refining and owning new ideas. The ideas we adopt fastest are the ones we feel invested in, familiar with and responsible for. Solution Questions engage buyers and give them these opportunities for co-creating alternatives and ideas.

Like the other types of DISCOVER Questions®, these are best used with the intent to explore customer needs (at any stage of the sales process). Asking Solution Questions early in the needs assessment phase of your sales process will be different from asking them after you already have specific ideas in mind to propose. Think back to the funnel described in chapter 9 and to the appropriate sequencing of questions in a conversational flow moving from very broad needs assessment to a narrower focus on the buyer's need for your product. Note the differences as you review these examples of Solution Questions.

> **The ideas we adopt fastest are the ones we feel invested in, familiar with and responsible for.**

Examples of Solution Questions

Broad Needs, For Use Early in the Needs Assessment

- What do your customers ask you to do differently?

- If you could start all over again, knowing then what you do now, what would you do differently?

- What alternatives have you already considered?

- Describe your "Plan B" and how you'll adjust if your current plan is not approved?

- What do your competitors do that you've considered copying?

Narrow Needs, For Use Late in the Needs Assessment

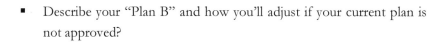

- What are your thoughts about mapping out a mock transition plan to get a feel for what would be involved?

- Let me get your initial reaction to this idea…

- How open are you to considering a proposal from me to address the needs you've described?

- I think we can help you adjust what you're already doing and improve the overall results. Which is more appealing for you – making small, incremental improvements or taking an entirely new approach?

- How do you feel about shifting the transport route to include supply options from two additional warehouses?

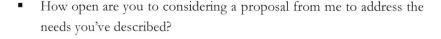

The key difference between questions used early in the conversation to probe broad needs vs. questions used later in the conversation is this – early in the assessment phase, Solution Questions should be crafted to elicit ideas from the buyer while later Solution Questions are used to introduce and test ideas from the seller.

Solution Questions to Elicit Buyer Ideas

Keeping this sequence will save the seller from prematurely pitching products which may or may not be a good solution. Even when a seller is absolutely certain he has exactly the right solution for the buyer, it is advantageous to slow down and help the buyer discover this truth for herself. When a seller leapfrogs over the steps of awareness, interest and desire in the buyer's process, he loses sales.

Additionally, when a buyer goes through a process of self-discovery and has an opportunity to brainstorm about ideas and alternatives, there are other advantages.

One advantage is often overlooked. Buyers enjoy this process! They appreciate sellers who challenge them to think and to stretch beyond the status quo. Recent research by the Conference Board and the Sales Executive Council quantifies this profound shift in buyer habits and preferences. Buyers expect sellers to be knowledgeable and to offer fresh, informed perspectives. Being an informed seller does not mean you have to be an expert. It does mean you need to be competent in asking questions to surface new ideas. But they don't have to be your own ideas!

You will never know as much about your buyer's business or personal needs as the buyer himself does. Using Solution Questions to extract and stir up ideas from the buyer is a smart strategy for creating value, and it doesn't cost a dime.

One buyer, considering the purchase of refurbished farm equipment, described his seller this way. "I'm not in a position to buy this week. But as soon as I'm able to buy, it will be definitely be from him. He really made me think, and that helped me work out the details. He earned the sale because he understood what I was trying to do, and he helped me understand it, too."

BUYERS SAY... The questions asked by the equipment dealer were Solution Questions. He doesn't consider himself to be an expert on operating a large-scale farm, but he does interact with ranch owners and farmers enough to understand how busy they are, how many variables they must consider in making business decisions, and how significant the impact of any one purchase can be on the rest of a growing season.

With this empathy and understanding, the farm equipment dealer asks his buyers questions so they will make fully informed decisions instead of hasty ones. He is widely viewed as a resource and friend to farmers in his region because he interacts with buyers in this way.

From a practical perspective, the equipment dealer describes how looking at alternatives helps his business, too. In addition to selling refurbished equipment, he also rents equipment and can order new equipment for buyers. Looking at all the alternatives and probing a variety of ideas helps him to offer the right solution for each buyer. He relies heavily on repeat business and referrals, so he knows he can't **INSIDE THE SALES CALL** alienate buyers by selling them what they don't need.

Check out two Solution Questions this equipment dealer asked a buyer who came in to make a combine harvester purchase: "I could sell you that or I could rent it to you for a few weeks. What are you gonna do with it when you're not harvesting?" and "What other choices do you have for getting set up in time for harvest?"

These questions caused the buyer to pause, think through the alternatives and step back to consider the bigger picture. Ultimately, he did purchase a piece of refurbished equipment. But the real value came in the careful planning he put into the

> **The seller benefits when the buyer is thinking strategically.**

purchase. Busy buyers often get so focused on tactical fixes and getting "to do" items checked off their lists that they forget to consider the bigger picture and broader implications. Solution Questions are refreshing and valuable because they remind buyers to think more strategically.

At the same time, the seller also benefits when the buyer is thinking strategically. This opens up possibility thinking, broadening the buyer's mindset so he or she is not overly focused on here and now, the way things are. Thinking more expansively means thinking more inclusively, considering new vendors and new products. That kind of thinking leads to sales opportunities.

Solution Questions to Introduce Seller Ideas

Solution Questions asked later in a needs assessment may also result in progressive permissions. A buyer who agrees to hearing your ideas, meeting again to discuss your proposal, being open to consider an incremental improvement... well, that's a buyer who is primed to buy.

Having said that, there is a counter balance to consider. Yes, Solution Questions can be used to set up a sales opportunity. But they are misused if that's all you do with them. In Chapter 10, we covered "Questions to Avoid" and defined the difference between influencing, persuading and manipulating. If a seller's questions come across as self-serving to slickly maneuver the buyer into a corner, then those questions will seem manipulative and unhelpful to the buyer. Instead of advancing the sale, this misguided approach will derail the sale.

One certain way to lose ground with Solution Questions is to jump straight to the ones that should be asked later in the interview. Until you learn broad-based business needs, it isn't yet time to drill down. These later questions should be used for shifting the conversation from the broadest needs of the buyer to the buyer's narrower needs for your product.

If, on top of that, you add closed-ending phrasing in front of these questions, you will transform them into something that sounds too tricky. Buyers feel Solution Questions like "What are your thoughts about ordering in bulk to cut costs?" create value and make them think. But phrasing like "Wouldn't you agree it's a good idea to order in bulk and cut costs?" diminishes the value of the question and causes buyers to feel sellers are trying to back them into a corner.

Well-crafted questions build trust and rapport. Keeping both the purpose of the question and the intent to understand buyer needs in mind will keep a seller on course so rapport is established and trust is built, even with just a few questions. But sellers must be vigilant so they do not accidentally slip into sloppy phrasing that sounds manipulative and erodes trust.

Developing the discipline to ask questions with intent and purpose is what will differentiate you from sellers who use questions indiscriminately. It takes time, patience and practice to master this skill and to recognize what will keep you in the driver's seat, steering conversations with finesse. Over time, though, you will find what many sellers have discovered – this is the most effective way possible to sell strategically and meet buyer needs. If that's what you're aiming for, then Solution Questions will be of particular importance to you because they are perceived by buyers to be of such high value when handled appropriately.

Look back at the Solution Question examples early in this chapter. In your second look, cull out the ways these examples lend themselves to broadening a buyer's point of view, to planting seeds of new ideas and to building progressive permissions for presenting possible solutions. Put yourself in the buyer's shoes and imagine what it would be like for a seller to ask you these questions instead of the usual fare.

The purpose of Solution Questions is to introduce alternatives or new ideas. This is exactly what modern buyers are demanding of sellers. Getting comfortable and competent with Solution Questions will make you an asset to every buyer you encounter.

CHAPTER 16
Consequence Questions

The C in DISCOVER Questions® stands for Consequence Questions. The purpose of these questions is to call attention to potential risks or challenges.

This type of question is one some sellers choose to avoid due to a misunderstanding about how buyers will respond when their attention is called to a potential risk or challenge. It's a common misperception of sellers to think buyers will resent being asked to think or talk about something unpleasant or uncomfortable.

The truth is sellers who never talk about anything negative with their buyers are sellers who are indifferent. Sales is not meant to be an endless stream of happy talk. It is naïve

> **Buyers want sellers to show them the good, the bad and the ugly.**

and ineffective to sell with rose-colored glasses. When a seller isn't realistic and doesn't take into account the buyer's risks and challenges, the seller is bound to make mistakes that could be costly for the buyer.

What's more, buyers want sellers to show them the good, the bad and the ugly. Buyers rely most on sellers who are candid and honest in their assessments. (See The 12 Dimensions of Trust in Chapter 1.) Buyers want sellers to provide knowledgeable advice, consultation and information they can't get anywhere else. Sellers who ignore the risks and challenges buyers are facing fail to meet the high standard modern buyers have set for sellers.

In business, as in our personal lives, we can't avoid potential risks, consequences of decisions we make, and day-to-day challenges. A seller who avoids talking about those things is a seller who isn't genuinely motivated to help the buyer. A seller who ignores those risks and challenges altogether is one who is destined to disappoint the buyer. Why? Because modern buyers expect sellers to keep them fully informed.

What these sellers are really saying is they are uncomfortable talking about the downsides of doing business. Frankly, they do not care enough about the buyer to have these deeper level conversations.

Let me illustrate this with a story. While grocery shopping one Saturday, I observed a little girl and her mother walking through the aisles. I enjoyed watching them because the little girl, who was about three years old, reminded me what it was like when my daughters were young. She was brimming with unbridled curiosity, asking her mom a stream of questions like "why do we eat yogurt?" and "why is yogurt good for my bones?" Her mother was patient and sweet with her, taking each question as it came and educating her as they made their way through the store.

Coincidentally, they left the store just as I did. There was another woman approaching them from the parking lot, perhaps a family friend or an aunt. The little girl saw the other woman and was very excited. She was so excited she darted out into the parking lot to race toward this woman.

She dashed right in front of an oncoming SUV. Fortunately, the driver slammed on his brakes and averted a tragedy. But it was a close call. The mother's response was to begin scolding the little girl. Understandably, the mother was highly emotional as she alternated between screaming and crying and hugging her daughter. At one point she even shook her daughter a little bit, staring straight into her eyes and saying loudly "you could have been killed!"

That's when the other woman censured the mother, saying "Stop! You're scaring her!" Before it was all over with, in these few seconds of intense drama, the little girl was crying, the mother was trembling, and the other woman was trying to manage the emotions of everyone involved.

As I drove home, I wondered what I would have done in the same situation. I think I would've reacted the same way the mother did. And I don't think that's a bad thing. Yes, the mother scared the little girl. That was undoubtedly the point. She scared her with the intention of preventing her from being in harm's way in the future. She cared enough about her child to express something negative, to show her something terrible, and to make a point that was important for the little girl to understand.

By doing so, she may have saved her life.

Consequence Questions Expose Risks

This is what we do when we care about people. We try to prevent them from getting hurt. We provide information to show them something they may not know or understand. We do not dodge the hard truths. We support them by clearly educating them about all the possibilities, even the ones that are frightening. We do this even though it would be easier to stick to light-hearted conversation and pleasantries.

Consequence Questions help us reveal potential risks to our buyers. We don't bring up potential risks simply to advance our own sales agenda. Instead, guided by our intention to understand and help our buyers, we reveal risks because we don't want our buyers to be blindsided by a danger they don't yet see.

Using questions to reveal risks keeps a seller from over-stating the potential danger. It's a seller's job to call attention to the possible risk or consequence, not to fully analyze and project it.

Remember, buyers are busy people. They are taxed with multiple priorities. Considering a purchase of your product is only one of many responsibilities they juggle on any given day. Any time you can help make a buyer's job easier, you differentiate yourself from other sellers and create value, repositioning yourself favorably in the buyer's eyes.

Because the buyer is busy, she might miss the potential risks you see. Never assume a buyer has already seen and dealt with risk. Instead, ask about it. If the buyer is aware of the situation, you will demonstrate empathy and understanding of the situation. If the buyer is not aware

> **If sellers don't bring attention to discomfort, they can't expect to sell solutions for it.**

of the risk, you will help prevent an accident. Alternately, if the buyer is aware but has avoided dealing with the risk, you will be the voice of reason who helps her through the unpleasant reality of the situation.

There is no downside to calling attention to potential risk, only an inexplicable apprehension for sellers. People change direction and make purchases when they are uncomfortable, at risk or in need. If sellers don't bring attention to discomfort, they can't expect to sell solutions for it.

There's a little bit of sales psychology operating here, too. Many people are motivated by fear of pain more than they are motivated by hope of gain. It's why healthy diet and exercise programs, the prescription for a longer life, aren't readily embraced by everyone all throughout their lives. But, some make drastic changes after a health scare when blood pressure rises dangerously or a mild heart attack serves as a wake-up call. Fear inspires action that wasn't taken before the close call drew attention to the risk.

Calling attention to a potential risk isn't a manipulative sales tactic. It will seem that way, though, if you exaggerate the risk or paint a dramatically bleak picture. A single question to make a buyer think is far more effective and will keep the risk in proportion to the buyer's own situation.

Advertisements for life insurance policies do a good job of using make-you-think Consequence Questions to starkly call attention to potential risk. Numerous companies use campaigns posing a question like "What will happen to your loved ones if you die tomorrow?"

While the question may seem heavy-handed, it is effective in making a prospect stop and think about the potential risk of inaction. The question does exactly what it is meant to do. It serves the purpose of calling attention to a potential risk.

Consequence Questions Reveal Risks

Here are five examples of Consequence Questions that are less dramatic but equally effective in giving a buyer pause so he or she can consider a potential risk:

- What will the impact be if you do not achieve your sales goal?

- Who is affected and how are they affected when production and shipping delays create this kind of backlog?

- Which of your competitors poses the greatest threat to your current market position?

- Tell me about your concerns – for yourself and for the business – if you don't deliver on deadline.

- What are the ramifications of proceeding before you have all the grant money in place?

Consequence Questions Reveal Challenges

Consequence Questions are also used to understand the challenges a buyer is experiencing. Within every challenge is a looming risk – what happens if this challenge is not overcome? Consequence Questions can help a seller to fully explore and understand a buyer's challenge and, by doing so, prepare a solution to minimize or eliminate the challenge and associated risk.

Here are five examples of Consequence Questions used to surface and understand the buyer's current challenges.

- What is standing in your way of reaching that goal?

- Describe the obstacles you are dealing with.

- What challenges have others encountered when they took on a project like this one?

- What is your most urgent or pressing problem with this project?

- As you introduce this change initiative, how could these unaddressed issues resurface as barriers on down the road?

Challenges get suppressed in the workplace and in highly competitive settings. You may have buyers who know, deep down, what difficulties to expect. But they may not have others they can discuss challenges with openly. Ignoring the challenges won't make them disappear. When you step in as a sounding board and resource for addressing challenges, you become more than just another seller.

Getting Comfortable with Consequence Questions

If you are troubled by the idea of asking questions to probe pain, reveal risks and check on challenges, consider one more aspect of these questions. Consequence Questions

> You are doing something for your buyer, not to your buyer.

are only one of eight types of question. You won't ask this type of question in every meeting nor of every buyer. You will ask this type of question when the situation warrants it and when you have already built trust with the buyer.

Think about the people you trust in your personal life. One reason you trust them is because you know they "have your back." They do not stand by and watch you make poor choices. Instead, they offer advice and call your attention to potentially hazardous situations. You do the same for them.

It's the same with buyers. Asking Consequence Questions provides a service. You are doing something **for** your buyer, not **to** your buyer.

When interviewed about questions asked during sales calls, buyers expressed gratitude for Consequence Questions. They acknowledged that the seller was not obligated to ask questions which would potentially surface unpleasant issues or negative reactions. They appreciated the concern shown when sellers did ask. In sales meetings where a risk or challenge loomed like an 800-pound gorilla but was ignored, buyers and sellers alike expressed awareness that there was something missing and something awkward about the meeting.

As you begin working with the eight discrete purposes of DISCOVER Questions®, you may initially be confused by some that seem similar. It is not uncommon for sellers to forget the difference between Issue Questions and Consequence Questions. They both surface and probe concerns a buyer may have. However, there is one key difference. Going back to the purpose of these two types of questions will help you distinguish one from the other.

Issue Questions probe or avoid problems in a relationship between the seller and buyer. Consequence Questions call attention to potential risks or challenges the buyer is facing. In other words, Issue Questions are related to problems caused by or involving the seller. But Consequence Questions are problems the seller is not involved in directly.

If your fear of asking Consequence Questions prevents you from doing asking them, ask yourself these Consequence Questions:

- What is the impact when my buyers are not motivated to buy?

- If I lose business to a seller who is not afraid of asking these questions, what's the long-term impact on my income and job security?

- Which would be worse: Asking an uncomfortable question to move past a hurdle? Or not asking and continuing to be stuck and unable to advance the sale?

By asking these questions, you can better understand the potential consequences of your own actions. Armed with this insight, you can make more informed choices. The same is true for your buyers. Asking Consequence Questions is a way to genuinely help them.

CHAPTER 17
Outcome Questions

The O in DISCOVER Questions® stands for Outcome Questions. The purpose of these questions is to learn about desired outcomes.

You can breathe a sigh of relief if you are a seller who is still not comfortable with asking Consequence Questions. You will like Outcome Questions and probably use this type with your buyers already. These are, by their very nature, "feel good" questions

> **Talking about desired outcomes gives buyers a chance to share their dreams with others.**

that make your buyers smile. Talking about desired outcomes gives buyers a chance to share their dreams with others.

Outcome Questions inquire about a buyer's hopes, needs, plans, goals, ideals or visions of the future. When a seller knows what a buyer would like to accomplish, the seller's proposal will be far more inspirational and compelling than it is without this insight.

This is one reason why sellers should start with broad questions at the top of the funnel and focus on what matters most to each individual buyer (see chapters 4 and 9). If you don't know what the buyer's goal is, you limit your own selling effectiveness. When sellers prioritize efficiency over effectiveness, they miss out on information enabling them to turn features into compelling benefits with relevance for each buyer.

Here's how it happens. A seller, burdened by a busy schedule and scrambling to reach quota, takes shortcuts. Instead of asking questions about the individual buyer or the buyer's business, the seller sees those questions as an extravagant luxury she cannot afford the time to ask. So she goes straight to questions about the buyer's narrower goal or need for the product she sells.

It's the difference between asking "what would you like to achieve in your business this year?" and "what quantity of my product do you need in a typical year?"

This is significant. There's really nowhere else to go after you gather the information on potential need for your product – all the seller can do now is offer generic features and presumed benefits. The pitch has no customization other than quantity. There is nothing inspirational, and the proposal will be no more compelling than a manipulation like price reduction or special promotion can make it.

By contrast, a seller who can attach to the big picture goal of the buyer has so much more to work with. If the business goal were, for example, to increase market share and overtake the top spot within five years, then the seller would be able to show the link between her product and how buying it helps, in some way, to move the business closer to that top spot.

Without an understanding of where the business or individual buyer wants to be, the seller is merely peddling product. The most effective sellers aim higher, operating as agents of change and inspiring by telling stories about how they can help their buyers reach their goals. None of that is possible without asking Outcome Questions.

> A seller who can attach to the big picture goal of the buyer has so much more to work with.

These examples of Outcome Questions are all appropriate as "top of the funnel" questions, inviting a buyer to provide expansive and broad answers related to more than the product purchase. Notice the key words that make Outcome Questions easy to identify – hopes, dreams, plans, goals, visions, ideals. Synonyms for any of these words would identify Outcome Questions just as definitively.

Outcome Questions are easy to categorize because they are always future-focused. Every Outcome Question looks toward the future state the buyer would like to achieve.

Examples of Outcome Questions

- With this initiative, what is the desired outcome?

- What does success look like?

- Describe the long-term vision for the project.

- Where do you hope to be a year from now?

- What are you forecasting for next quarter?

- How do you plan to achieve those goals?

- What would your dream job be?

A Powerful Pairing

When a seller pairs Outcome Questions with follow-up Consequence Questions, a fuller picture emerges. With this information, a seller can see how the solution she offers can dually help a buyer achieve his goal and avoid a consequence related to not reaching that goal. Here are three examples of Outcome and Consequence Questions that have been paired together to reveal a more complete picture.

Seller: What is your objective for joining a gym? *Outcome Question*

Buyer: I'd like to drop two dress sizes before my cousin's wedding.

Seller: How will you feel if you don't get there? *Consequence Question*

Buyer: Really bad. That's why I'm here. I need help.

Seller: What is the ideal brand you'd like to convey? *Outcome Question*

Buyer: That we are dedicated to our customers, going far beyond what others do in order to make people feel right at home when they stay with us.

Seller: What currently prevents 100% of your guests from leaving with that impression? *Consequence Question*

Buyer: We had some gaps in service due to poor hiring decisions and a training issue. We've fixed that now, but we have to work harder to repair the damage to our image.

INSIDE THE SALES CALL

Seller: Tell me about your growth plans. *Outcome Question*

Buyer: We're expanding into the northeast region over the next three years. Once we have a strong foothold there with our upscale concept, we will begin updating stores in other regions where the consumer demographics indicate a good fit.

Seller: What challenges are you anticipating as you move forward with this plan? *Consequence Question*

Buyer: I don't expect our competition to just roll over on this. They'll respond aggressively. They may even enter into the markets where we already dominate and try to gain share here while we're focusing up there.

The question pairs reveal so much more than a single question does. And these two types of questions fit naturally together, lending themselves to smooth conversational flow. If a seller is guided by his own curiosity, these follow-up Consequence Questions are to be expected. In fact, considering the buyer responses to the initial Outcome Questions, follow-up questions are only natural. It would be awkward not to follow up with these questions to round out the conversation.

In the interest of saving time and avoiding uncomfortable subjects, some sellers avoid Consequence Questions. Likewise, some sellers leap straight into Consequence Questions and forego Outcome Questions to save time and to make the buyer's pain point the primary focus of the needs assessment. As a seller using DISCOVER Questions®, you should use your best discretion in each sales call. You know your customers and your own style better than others. These various types of questions are meant to be mixed and matched in whatever way best suits the situation.

Let me reiterate this point. There is no absolute required for DISCOVER Questions® to boost your sales effectiveness. A single question, crafted to be purposeful and with the intent to understand your buyer, will have an impact. Asking eight different types of questions doesn't have to happen in a single conversation. The questions themselves should not dictate what comes next in any conversation. Instead, your own interest in the buyer's needs and situation will direct you to ask the types of questions that will yield the information you are seeking.

Knowing about and developing agility with eight types of questions starts with fully understanding the purpose of all eight types. Even though some types will be more familiar and comfortable to you, stretch to get equally adept at using the other types, too. When you use all eight types of DISCOVER Questions® you will differentiate yourself from others sellers and become the one seller buyers actually WANT to talk to.

CHAPTER 18
Value Questions

The V in DISCOVER Questions® stands for Value Questions. The purpose of these questions is to prioritize and clarify what's most important to the buyer.

In sales, making assumptions is never a good idea. Ask any seasoned sales professional about a memorable mistake (s)he's made with a buyer and you'll likely hear a story that starts with an assumption.

The most damaging assumptions of all are the ones that result in viewing or treating all buyers the same. Overlooking what each individual personally values drastically decreases your selling effectiveness. This is a tempting trap for sellers (and marketers) to fall into without even realizing it. It happens when we let what's common amongst our buyers become the only thing we pay attention to about our buyers. It also happens when we think more about what's being purchased than about whom is doing the purchasing.

> In sales, making assumptions is never a good idea.

An airport shoe shiner told me he doesn't pay attention to people's faces or bodies, only to their feet. He can recognize a regular Monday morning traveler by the shoes he's wearing week after week but not by his facial features. The problem is when someone gets a new pair of shoes the shoe shiner doesn't recognize it's a regular, returning customer. He misses out on tips because as soon as the pair of shoes changes, he doesn't deliver the higher level of service and friendly banter he reserves for regulars he recognizes.

Although this may sound like an extreme example, think about all the places where this is commonplace, where buyers are looked at only in the context of what they're buying. At a local coffee shop, you aren't known as a working mother who's completing her master's degree. Instead, you are "the skinny iced green tea, blended, grande, no cream." If you run into your barista at the gym on a Sunday afternoon, neither of you will recognize the other.

We also lump like buyers into categories and make assumptions about them based on these arbitrary groupings. This begins with industry and/or company segmentation of buyers. You end up with sales channels like retail, wholesale and co-op. Layer in internal groupings like major accounts and call center accounts. Don't forget the informal classifications, too, like "bread and butter" vs. "growth" accounts. Pretty

> **Buyers resent being categorized and labeled.**

soon, we've put so many labels on our buyers that we think we know everything we need to about them before we even know their names!

These labels lead to generalities. Those generalities lead to "one size fits all" marketing materials, sales pitches and solutions. The individual buyer, the one who is actually making the purchasing decision, is overlooked. Sellers don't realize this is happening. They believe superficial social niceties are adequate substitutes for genuinely knowing the unique needs of every individual buyer. So they continue operating on these false assumptions and wonder what happened when they lose the business to a competitor.

Buyers resent being categorized and labeled. They ignore mass mailings, generic e-mails, canned pitches and over-scripted sales presentations. The sales and marketing departments may be spot on in identifying what should be appealing to a particular target audience of buyers, but the "one size fits all" approach for delivering the message will cause it to fall flat.

Rule #1 in Selling: Never Assume

Illustration 7

That's because sellers end up tripping all over the assumptions embedded in a process like this. Right information, wrong delivery.

Even when the assumptions are accurate, a buyer will be unimpressed because there is no personalization and no involvement of the buyer.

You've experienced this as a buyer. Think about the times when you've been in front of a salesperson who is reciting a pitch that's irrelevant and uninteresting to you. You feel marginalized, maybe even invisible, as your obvious discomfort and annoyance is disregarded. If you endure the pitch long enough, the seller's presumptuousness in telling you what you need will become downright degrading.

Sadly, professional sellers, including those in B2B settings, skirt the line of doing this, too. Maybe it happens because you sell to clients who all do the same type of work. You may reason, for example, all IT Project Leads have similar education and professional backgrounds, as well as having common needs because they deal with a common set of problems. Or maybe your clients are all HR Managers or all CFOs or all Operations Directors or all Sales VPs… as soon as you add the word "all" in front of your assigned account and prospect list, you're doomed to make dangerous assumptions.

> **Value Questions are the best possible replacement for assumptions.**

Connect on an Individual Level

There's only one remedy. Step back from the prepackaging of your account list, priority leads or buyer personas and think of each buyer as a unique individual. Start by considering what is important to each person – not what is the reason they should want your product (that will come later), but what it is that matters to this human being.

Value Questions will help you to identify what matters. Value Questions are the best possible replacement for assumptions. At a minimum, sellers can use Value Questions to check their own assumptions and to gauge the importance of each proven assumption. Even if similar buyers do value the very same things, they will value those things in different proportions depending on life circumstances and current priorities.

Sellers who do not ask Value Questions routinely report that they don't see a need to ask these questions. They don't see a need because their view of buyers is clouded by assumptions.

Here are three examples of sellers who relied on prevailing assumptions and learned, the hard way, that assumptions are not reliable.

Assumption #1 – What Other Sellers Say is True

A media sales representative was reassigned to the automotive category. She had heard (and believed) all auto dealers were pressed for time, short on advertising funds, and made decisions based on proven ROI. So she put together a slick presentation that took just 90 seconds to present, highlighted dramatic cost savings and projected better-than-average return on investment. Imagine her surprise when five GMs flatly rejected her offer within seconds of the individual presentations she made to each of them. She was stumped.

In debrief meetings with these buyers, we learned how the presentations completely missed the mark. While it was true auto dealers felt pressed for time, short on advertising funds and pressured to deliver strong ROI on every ad dollar spent, these factors alone weren't going to determine what advertising they purchased. More important factors were left undiscovered because the ad rep skipped needs assessment and even rapport building. She over-relied on other sellers instead.

Complicating the matter, all five GMs felt the presentation was insulting and presumptuous. They resented being viewed so impersonally. The fifth one had already heard from the first about the presentation, and he was doubly offended because he considered his luxury car dealership to be in a different class entirely.

One simple Value Question would have given the seller more to work with and would have enabled her to customize her presentation to each buyer. Value is personal, and if you don't personalize your sales offering you run the risk of being the stereotypical seller who buyers intentionally avoid.

Assumption #2 – The Need for My Product is Obvious

A pharmaceutical rep visits doctors' offices to present new products. Obviously, she reasons, doctors write prescriptions for patients who have the matching diagnoses. The need for her products is apparent, and doctors who specialize in treating certain ailments should be eager to spend time with her learning about these new prescription drugs.

An experienced telemarketer sells replacement windows. The need for these, the sales trainer explains, is obvious in homes where the heat of summer and the cold of winter drive up utility costs, especially in homes that do not have double-pane windows. The replacement windows ought to sell themselves because they will pay for themselves in just 5 years.

A seasoned technology sales consultant sells a software system for companies introducing or upgrading their eLearning platforms. His system is both the easiest to learn and the least expensive option available for mid-size, multiple location businesses. It's exactly what every Training Manager needs… or so our seller believes.

All three of these sellers felt the products they offered were "no brainer" sales. They truly believed the need for their products was so obvious that the sales call would be "just a formality." Each inherited an established account list or a set of pre-qualified leads to pursue. Each one believed they simply needed to connect the buyer with the product in order for the sale to be completed. As they called their clients and prospects, they routinely opened with assumptions like these:

"Yes, I'd like to know when Dr. Silverman takes non-patient appointments. I'll be stopping by with product samples and will need to speak with him directly."

"I'm calling today because your home is long overdue for replacement windows that will save energy and enhance the ambiance of your home. We will have an estimator in your neighborhood Wednesday and Thursday next week. What time would you like to claim on his schedule?"

INSIDE THE SALES CALL

"Thank you for your interest in our new eLearning platform. We typically need 30 days to spec your needs, build your customized content and set up your interface. How soon are you planning to get started?"

There are two things missing in these sales openings. The first is alignment with the buyer's process (see chapter 3). These sellers assumed the buyers were further along in the buying process than they actually were. Buyers become aware and interested before they desire a product and take action to acquire it. Sellers who assume buyers are ready to take action fail to build interest and desire. Sales do not advance when sellers get ahead of buyers.

The other missing ingredient in these openings is value. Sellers have assumed there is an obvious or inherent value in what they are offering. They expect the buyer to already have a full understanding of and appreciation for this value. But it doesn't work that way. Even when a buyer acknowledges a practical need for a product, the buyer's desire will intensify if value is magnified and clarified. Explaining why a buyer should get this particular product at this exact moment in time requires linking the purchase to something the buyer values.

Since value is personal, a seller must ask Value Questions in order to appeal to an individual buyer. The generic benefits like "save energy," "get free product samples" and "easy to learn" don't compel action. At best, they create interest and possibly build desire. It takes a direct hit on the value that matters most to an individual buyer to inspire a sale.

For the window replacement telemarketer, the number of appointments she set jumped dramatically when she began asking "What appeals to you most about the idea of double pane replacement windows?" This Value Question revealed whether buyers would be motivated by the ease of cleaning, the updated look, the energy efficiency, the cost savings or the improved home value. Once the seller knew what would be most appealing, she could convey relevant benefits and truly build desire.

The need for your product is never obvious to a buyer. That's because buyers have more options that are more readily available to them than ever before in history. Further, they do not consider your products to be significantly different from the ones offered by your competitors. Until you make the need for your solution obvious by linking it to what the buyer values, you are at risk of losing the sale, thanks to your own assumptions.

Assumption #3 – What the Buyer Valued Before Hasn't Changed

It took several years and an egregious and embarrassing error, but this manufacturer's representative now understands how a buyer's priorities can change over time.

Like many sellers, he followed a sales process with a needs assessment phase. He asked good questions during the initial needs assessment and became well acquainted with the owner of a family hardware store that had been in business for over 55 years.

Of particular interest was the owner's pride in the family history with the business. It had been started by his grandfather, passed on to his father and was now his to operate. He hoped to outlast the encroachment of big box stores and remain competitive through personal service and customer loyalty. Ultimately, what he wanted most of all was to retire early like his father had and to pass the business on to his two sons.

The seller visited the store quarterly on his route through this part of his geographic territory. He talked up the American Dream and the merits of family business during each visit. Knowing the business owner would be most motivated to compete with the Goliaths by his desire to leave a profitable business to his sons, the seller prefaced all his recommendations with that same story and central value.

So far, so good.

But the seller, even 10 years into the relationship, assumed the buyer's priorities would remain the same. They didn't. The business owner realized the interests of his sons, now in high school, were not aligned with running the hardware store. One was a gifted musician who earned a scholarship to study at a prestigious school. The other was interested in studying law and was **INSIDE THE SALES CALL** recognized as a top scholar. He was being recruited by numerous universities. This buyer's priorities, value and dream changed.

In response to these changes, the hardware store owner decided to keep the business going just long enough to put his boys through college. He now valued short-term profit over long-term business stability and reputation.

Because he never took the time to check back on the business owner's needs or primary value, the seller knew none of this. He wondered why the personnel in the store seemed younger and more inexperienced. He also noticed the owner was less aggressive in promoting the business, putting fewer signs in the windows and offering fewer special offers in-store. But he did not probe the reasons for the changes he observed.

When the seller heard the older son was graduating from high school, he decided to give him the gift of a new, customized sign for the store. He had the sign replicated but changed "3 generations" to "4 generations." The new signage was delivered directly to the home, addressed to the son who had graduated.

Unfortunately, the timing was all wrong. Although he fully supported his grandsons' talents and interests, the second-generation owner of the business was deeply disappointed by their lack of interest in the family business. He was at the home when the gift arrived during a particularly sensitive conversation about this very subject. The son who received the gift thought the signage was a coercive tactic meant to make him feel guilty and give up his own pursuits.

Who's responsible for this turn of events? You could argue that the owner should have told the seller. But why would he? No questions were asked, and routine sales calls didn't lend themselves to sharing this information. You could say it was an honest mistake or that the seller's good intentions ought to count for something. But there were ample opportunities to make observations and ask about changes – after all, this change in plans had been building for years.

When the dust settled, the seller lost his job. The angry call to his company's VP of Sales was not the first. Other customers' complaints about his lack of interest had been mounting. The seller had become complacent, serving his accounts as an order taker instead of selling his accounts like a professional. When sellers conduct a single needs assessment and then use outdated or stale information for the long term, this outcome is not unusual.

In his next job, the seller vowed to remain focused on customer needs and values. He spends time in every meeting asking about what has changed and checking his own assumptions. He is observant about changes in the businesses he visits and asks about the significance of changes he observes. His current customers consider him to be a true resource.

Buyers Get Clarity, Too

Knowing what your buyers value influences what you sell them, how you interact with them and what you do for them. Assumptions based on stale information will lead to costly relationship mistakes and missed sales opportunities. It doesn't take much time at all to check in on what a buyer values, and the payoff for doing so is well worth the investment of time and effort.

When you spend time exploring what the buyer values, there is another benefit, too. You might not be the only one who needs clarity. Sometimes, busy buyers haven't recently reflected on what matters currently or what matters most. They, too, may be operating on auto-pilot, making choices and buying decisions out of habit or in response to outdated perceptions. Getting clarity about what is important in the present can cause buyers to make shifts they otherwise would not make.

Examples of Value Questions

To ascertain what your buyer currently values and in what proportion they value one thing over another, you can ask Value Questions like these.

- You've described several goals for the coming year. Of these, which one is the most important to achieve?

- How is your performance measured?

- What does it mean to you, personally, when your customers report higher levels of satisfaction?

- Help me understand why this is so important to your firm.

- Given all the changes in the competitive landscape, what shifts in priorities are you hearing from corporate?

- For you, what are the absolute "must haves" in add-on options? What are the "nice to haves?"

- Tell me about what drives you to excel in your work.

- You've outlined seven changes you'd like to see. I'd be interested in knowing the hierarchy you see in how they relate to each other.

- Of the features outlined in my proposal, which ones are of least importance to you?

- I understand your position and what you're asking us to do. Please explain for me what the underlying motivations are for this request.

The purpose of Value Questions is to prioritize and clarify what's most important to the buyer. Questions like these prevent a seller from making assumptions or offering irrelevant and uninspiring features to the buyer. Once value (which is inherently personal – see Chapter 4) has been determined, a seller can zero in on which benefits will be most compelling for the buyer.

Value Questions help make the initial sale, and they ensure high levels of service and satisfaction for the duration of a buyer/seller relationship **if** the seller checks in frequently to stay current on what is of primary importance to the buyer.

When buyers are asked about the way they perceive Value Questions, they express appreciation for the seller who understands what matters most to them. Additionally, they report that these questions have made them re-evaluate their own priorities and focused them with newfound clarity.

Like most types of DISCOVER Questions®, Value Questions create value for the buyer. The buyer doesn't have to wait for a solution in order to benefit from created value. Value is generated and accessed right in the moment when the question is asked. For a seller, this no-cost value creation is also advantageous because it differentiates him or her from all other sellers.

Of all eight types of DISCOVER Questions®, Value Questions are, in my estimation, the most important to understand and routinely use. For sellers with a true intent to understand their buyers' needs, Value Questions will become a part of nearly every sales encounter

CHAPTER 19
Example Questions

The E in DISCOVER Questions® stands for Example Questions. The purpose of these questions is to create a concrete example or contrast.

Put yourself in the buyer's shoes. As the moment of truth approaches, that moment when you will be required to make a decision about what to buy and how much to buy, how are you feeling?

You may be a little apprehensive or unsure about your next move. You know you will need to make a commitment very soon, but there are so many unanswered questions. Even though you've reviewed the options, done your due diligence in talking to multiple suppliers, run the numbers and outlined your next steps, a few pesky "what ifs?" are holding you back. Mainly, it's your own inability to fully envision what this change will look like.

As a buyer, perhaps you've experienced something like this. Home improvement contractors and designers say this is their greatest frustration – the inability of buyers to take the first steps because they can't grasp the final picture clearly enough to commit to the plan.

Example Questions help buyers by giving them something concrete, enabling them to see or understand what they will be asked to do or buy. Buyers feel more comfortable making a purchase once they are able to relate it to what is familiar.

This is why car sellers are so eager to put buyers behind the wheel for a test drive. Standing beside a car and looking at it simply isn't the same as being in the driver's seat and fully experiencing the new car smell, cushy seats, convenient cup holders, peppy acceleration, crystal clear sound, leg room and navigation system. It's the experience we buy, not the collection of metal and plastic parts.

No matter what you sell, you will sell more of it if your buyers can envision themselves "behind the wheel," using your product and experiencing

> **Give your buyers the added desire and confidence they need to take action.**

all the accompanying sensations and benefits. This is easier to build in to some sales presentations than others. If you sell a product or service directly to the end user, you have an advantage. But if you are not selling direct, the experience you must create is not going to be as sensory. Similarly, if you sell a product that has physical and well-understood sensory associations, you have an advantage over someone who sells intangibles.

Regardless of what you sell or who you sell it to, Example Questions can help you conjure concrete associations to give your buyers the added desire and confidence they need to take action. You could also paint visual pictures and tell stories to illustrate the experience for the buyer. This type of storytelling is extremely effective in selling. When you add Example Questions, you are engaging the buyer, too, in the storytelling. The buyer provides the concrete details for the story you weave together.

To prompt a buyer, use Example Questions asking for comparisons and contrasts. This is a good starting place for the type of thinking that calls specific details to mind. Additionally, this will remind your buyer and inform you about both favorable and unfavorable experiences. As you open up the memories associated with these comparisons, you'll also get insights into your buyers' experiences with your competitors or other vendors.

Examples of Example Questions

Consider these five Example Questions and what they yielded from the buyers.

Example Question 1

Seller: What differences were you able to track when you switched over

174

from your old phone system to the one you have now?

Buyer: Before we switched, everyone had to crowd into the conference room every morning to be on the tele-con with HQ. After the call, there was a lot of socializing and downtime. Now, people call in from their own desk and stay productive. Our order fulfillment rate before 10:00 a.m. has increased by 15% and we're buying a lot less coffee and donuts.

INSIDE THE SALES CALL

We get better quality on the speaker phones in the conference room, too. I hate having to lean in on a phone and repeat myself over and over again. Now we can sit anywhere in the conference room and carry on a decent conversation.

The rollover features on the new phones are pretty good, too. We don't leave customers hanging or waiting for someone to answer. We've got it programmed to get to a live human or to a voice mail after just 3 rings.

It was a lot of hassle to make the change, but I'm glad we did.

Example Question 2

Seller: Describe the contrast between what you expected and what you experienced when you refinanced last year.

Buyer: It wasn't nearly as bad as I thought it would be. The last time we refinanced, there were so many
INSIDE THE SALES CALL
hoops to jump through and constant stress. Since it is harder now to get a loan, I thought the whole process would be more difficult, too. My loan agent made it easy and kept us updated along the way which I really appreciated.

Example Question 3

Seller: Walk me through the pros and cons of sourcing local in the summer months vs. using the same supplier year-round.

Buyer: Just one positive, but it's a big one. Consumers think they want local produce. If they can't get it here, they'll be at their farmer's markets and shopping with other retailers. That's why we feel like we have to do it.

INSIDE THE SALES CALL

On the other hand, there's a lot of hassle and risk involved. Small local farms may not have the same quality and food safety standards. We can't count on a steady supply. What we get may not have made it into the cold chain fast enough so even though it looks good today it may go bad tomorrow.

The other problem is packaging. The weights are inconsistent and cheap packaging doesn't stay closed or display well. The produce managers would rather deal with a single supplier because it makes displays a lot more appealing.

It's a funny thing about what happens with sales, too. When we bring in local we get traffic increases, but our produce sales dip. People come in because we carry local, but then they don't buy it because it doesn't have the strong brand name or the same level of quality.

Example Question 4

Seller: How did your experience compare with the experience others described to you before you made the purchase?

Buyer: They painted a pretty picture, but they didn't deliver on it. You've heard "once burned, twice shy?" That's me. They told me I would get preferred customer status and my own direct service rep to handle any issues. That sounded pretty good. But it turns out my service rep is based overseas and has an accent I can't understand so good. Not only that, but my service rep hasn't even seen the software, so he

INSIDE THE SALES CALL

always has to pass me off to the tech team. That usually takes 30 minutes or more of being on hold.

I've had so many problems with this software. I don't even remember why I got it in the first place. That's why I'm starting over and plan to be a lot more careful this time.

Example Question 5

Seller: Once the transition has been completed, what will the major differences be?

Buyer: Actually, we have a complete checklist of 25 key differences. We mapped out what success would look like and this is what we all agreed upon. Doing this is what helped us pick a vendor because we used the checklist as our selection criteria, too. Internally, I had to set up this process just to sell my cross-functional teammates on the project. A lot of people couldn't understand the significance until we showed them all the differences and how it would impact people

INSIDE THE SALES CALL

across the organization. Here's the complete list.

Stay in the Driver's Seat

As you see in these sales scenarios, Example Questions invite lengthy and detailed responses. You won't typically get short answers to questions like these. What you will get is rich detail about a situation, context to understand your buyer's reluctance or underlying motivations, and numerous clues about what your buyer pays attention to and expects.

As you listen to responses to your Example Questions, pay close attention to both the content and the feeling your buyer is expressing (see chapter 11). When people share experiences and examples, they drop hints about back stories and breadcrumbs you can follow to get high value information. Use your natural curiosity to probe the clues you hear or sense. Other types of DISCOVER Questions® will enable you to ask follow-ups to fill in the gaps.

To avoid getting too much tangential information and irrelevant details, stay mindful of your central purpose. By asking questions, you steer the conversation. Follow up on the information and clues yielding useful and actionable information (see Chapter 10.) Don't get caught up in gossip or intrigue when you hear buyer stories. Keep yourself focused on understanding the buyer's needs, knowing you

> **Example Questions invite lengthy and detailed responses.**

will present a solution to meet those needs.

Buyer preferences, concerns, perceptions and experiences are vitally important to know about. They inform you on how you will need to present in order to be compelling, credible and effective.

There are times when a seller doesn't need quite so much detail and context. This may be the case when a long-term buyer/seller relationship has already been established. Example Questions used when a seller wishes to contain the volume of information should be constructed in a way that constricts or narrows what is being asked.

Craft Example Questions like these for times when you want to narrowly frame the conversation.

- Last year, you installed 2.0 and brought in our training team. When

3.0 launches next month, what should be replicated? Changed?

- You beta tested with two user groups. Which group is adopting faster and why?

- What's the difference in weekend sales when you promote with both print and online advertising vs. running in print alone?

- It's been six months since we shadowed and surveyed your front-line production workers. How have their levels of productivity and engagement changed since that initial boost?

- Describe your best month and your worst month for same-store sales numbers. What staffing differences are there in those months?

The purpose of Example Questions is to call to mind a concrete example or contrast. Rather than telling the buyer your own story to illustrate a specific point or bring to life an abstract idea, asking these questions gets the buyer to tell the story from his own point of view. Since no one's words are as believable to us as our own, the buyer begins selling himself as he builds the case for or against what he's describing.

When asked how they felt about Example Questions, buyers described feeling connected to sellers. By sharing their experiences and stories, buyers formed bonds with their sellers, just as we all do with people who are interested in us and actively listen to us. When sellers echoed buyers' stories back to them in proposals, buyers said it meant a great deal to them to be heard and understood.

To use Example Questions with maximum impact, the

savvy seller will pick up on what the buyer is talking himself into and ask follow-up questions to edify and magnify the elements of the story the seller can incorporate into her solution. When the buyer is helping you to advance the sale, you're on your way to a solid close.

CHAPTER 20
Rationale Questions

The R in DISCOVER Questions® stands for Rationale Questions. The purpose of these questions is to understand how a decision has been or will be made.

All too often, sellers know they are competing to win a buyer's business

> **There's a simpler way to win business when competing head-to-head**

but have no idea what it will take to come out on top. They do a lot of guess work and, thanks to their competitive zeal, may go overboard to offer price concessions and promotional extras that are not necessary.

There's a simpler way to win business when competing head-to-head. Asking Rationale Questions gives a seller insight into how the buyer will decide on a supplier.

Understanding How Decisions Will Be Made

As you read through this list of sample Rationale Questions, think about what it would mean to you if you had information like this before making a pitch to a buyer.

- As you compare the options, what will your top three decision criteria be?

- Who is involved in making this decision and how?

- What has led to your decision to consider us as a possible supplier at this time?

- What are the knockout factors that will cause you to decide against certain vendors?

- Aside from the stated decision criteria and apart from the named decision makers, who or what else will influence your decision?

Buyers appreciate when sellers ask them thoughtful Rationale Questions. These questions momentarily slow down the decision-making process and force the buyer to consider and declare what the criteria will be in making a decision. Without clarity, decision quality suffers.

When asked about the specific Rationale Questions they heard from sellers, buyers responded most favorably to questions that made them think about (and sometimes discuss with others) what was going on "behind the scenes." Bringing the decision process out into the open, buyers said, showed genuine interest on the part of the seller – interest demonstrating a desire to win the business and to get on the same page with the buyer. Some buyers described the questions they heard as strategic, analytical or smart. But the most common word used to describe Rationale Questions was "caring." Buyers felt the sellers asking these questions cared more than those who did not.

Understanding Previous Decisions

Rationale Questions can also be used to understand decisions that have already been made. Knowing how a buyer got to the current state can help a seller in future negotiations and sales presentations. However, when asking about past decisions, sellers should proceed with caution. Remember the purpose of these questions is to understand how a decision was made. That needs to come through in the way you phrase your question.

Asking about past decisions, if not done artfully, can put buyers on the defensive. It may sound like you are questioning the individual himself or his judgment. As soon as you are perceived as doing so, the defensive buyer may withdraw and look elsewhere for a more considerate seller.

Although buyers want to be challenged, they don't want to be put on the spot. Although they demand knowledge and expertise from a seller, they also want respect. A direct challenge to a buyer's decision or judgment may be construed as unhelpful rather than constructive. (Of course, you know your buyers best, so challenge each one in the way you know will be most effective.)

> **Although buyers want to be challenged, they don't want to be put on the spot.**

To avoid sounding like you are questioning the buyer's judgment, keep your primary intent top of mind. You are striving to understand the buyer and his or her needs. You are not having this conversation with the intention to score points by disproving something the buyer has already done. Keeping clear about your own intention will show through in how you ask a Rationale Question. Your tone will be open and curious, not judging.

What you say will be important, too. Do not use the word "why" in a Rationale Question. The word "why" immediately triggers a defensive response in some people. Don't ask "Why did you decide to...?" or "Why aren't you...?" Even if the reason why is what you actually want to know, rephrase these questions to eliminate the word "why."

The command statements introduced in chapter 8 will give you good replacement phrases so your Rationale Questions invite open responses and yield useful information despite this prohibition on the word "why."

Examples of Rationale Questions

Here are samples of Rationale Questions to probe a decision that has already been made. Remember, the tone should be open and interested as you ask questions like these.

- Please help me understand how you reached this decision.

- What was the process for reviewing your options and making this determination?

- Tell me about your evaluation and how it led you to this conclusion.

- What prompted this decision at this time?

- Considering the number of available options, I'm interested in hearing the back story about how you got to this point.

These questions may yield background information or process information you can use in the future. Sellers often pick up on buyer's remorse when they ask these questions in a non-threatening way. They also hear clues about what attracts the attention of decision makers and how to break through barriers they haven't been able to penetrate in the past.

One seller was frustrated because she felt she had a superior product and a good value proposition for a prospect. The buyer routinely accepted her proposals and seemed to be interested in the product offerings. But, time after time, the seller was disappointed when the business went to her

INSIDE THE SALES CALL

competitors.

After the sixth let down in a year, she asked the buyer to walk her through the decision-making process that had just taken place. The buyer did not hesitate. She explained there was a review panel and a set of criteria for any purchase over $10,000 due to corporate governance standards and auditing constraints. She shared how other vendors provided information relevant to each department represented on the panel while this seller directed her proposal only to her main contact. The buyer said she tried to fill in the blanks but couldn't go too far and show any sort of favoritism.

When the next proposal was solicited, the seller used more Rationale Questions to understand decision criteria and to find out who was serving on the review panel. Her proposal was accepted, and she has enjoyed a long-term relationship with this company ever since.

There is no need for sellers to compete blindly. Buyers don't mind sharing what will go into their decisions. After all, the buyer benefits when a seller provides all the germane information rather than bits and pieces that may not be of interest.

Rationale Questions help a seller to understand how a buyer's decision has been or will be made. With this insight, you will be able to differentiate your solution, maintain alignment with your buyer and compete for business more effectively.

PART III
SKILLS PRACTICE

You've now been equipped to use the eight types of DISCOVER Questions® that will make you the one seller buyers WANT to talk to. You've also read about techniques for connecting with buyers so you can advance the sale effectively and improve your close ratio and your customer retention.

Practice makes perfect. Sellers who take the time to practice and master these skills differentiate themselves from those who understand them but have not perfected their technique.

You'll enjoy the practice exercises and the support of the DISCOVER Questions® Community. Start here as soon as possible!

"The more I use these questions, the more popular I become. My customers constantly thank me and compliment me on the way I sell. My sales manager says she can't believe how much my numbers have improved. My book of business keeps growing every week. The only thing I'm doing differently this year is asking the 8 types of open-ended questions with the intention to uncover buyer needs. It really changes things."

CHAPTER 21
Becoming a Question Detective

It takes practice to develop competence with DISCOVER Questions® and to form solid connections with buyers. Reading this book is a first step, but the real work begins when you decide to put into practice what you've read about here.

Sellers who work with these principles and invest time to try, take risks, fail and try again report transformational change in the way they sell and in the results they get. Making that commitment is something only you can do for yourself. If you're up for it, this section of the book – these two remaining chapters – will give you the blueprint for success.

Most sellers can conceptually understand the eight different types of questions with just a little bit of review. You may already be at this point and don't feel an immediate need to practice. Trust those who have worked through this already – you will benefit from the skills practices offered here. The difference between conceptually understanding DISCOVER Questions® and being proficient and facile in using them is significant. It's like knowing there are four tires on a car vs. being the pit crew at the Daytona 500 who can change all four tires in 12 seconds flat.

This chapter focuses on honing your questioning skills. That includes recognizing different types of questions, improving poorly crafted questions, dissecting questions asked and what they yielded, and using questions to steer the conversation and advance the sale. You'll begin by becoming a question detective, analyzing questions asked and understanding the cause and effect behind every question asked and every answer given.

Chapter 22 is where you'll write your own DISCOVER Questions® to fit the buyers you work with and your own selling situations. In Chapter 22, you'll also practice staying true to your intent – writing broader questions to probe business needs and narrower questions to pinpoint the buyer's need for the product you're selling.

As an author, Deb Calvert welcomes questions from readers and will gladly coach you through any challenges you're experiencing as you start to use purposeful questions. Anyone who's read this much of the book deserves a little extra attention! Just email Deb at deb.calvert@peoplefirstps.com if you would like some one-to-one support.

Becoming a Question Detective

To become a question detective, you will need to sharpen your active listening skills. Doing the exercises suggested in this chapter will give you dual practice in both active listening and quality questioning. Remember, you need both skills in order to become more effective in meeting buyer expectations.

There are five progressive exercises here to stair step you into a heightened awareness about question construction and how asking better questions will yield better information.

Step 1: Listen to Interviews

Talk radio, post-game press conferences, late night TV, investigative news shows, celebrity red carpet events... All of these feature interviews conducted by experienced question askers. Listen to the way they construct their questions and pay attention to which questions generate the most information.

Here are seven items to note as you listen to interviews:

1. When interviewing actors who are promoting their latest movie or project, skilled interviewers tend to ask more closed-ended questions. This is because people with a set agenda don't really need open and inviting questions. They have certain talking points they will make regardless of what questions are asked. The closed-ended questions

are intentional because they are efficient and keep answers brief. This ensures two-way dialogue with the interviewer.

2. Investigative journalists on programs like *60 Minutes* and talk show hosts with a reputation for in-depth interviews (think Barbara Walters or Terry Gross) set the standard for asking open-ended and thought-provoking questions. Not every interviewer is capable of extracting as much emotion and truth as these talented few can.

3. Good interviewers are comfortable with silence. They don't try to fill in the gaps in a conversation. Once they've asked a question, they let it settle in instead of rephrasing or changing it. They never offer answers to their own questions either.

4. Good interviews progress from non-threatening topics to those that are more probing. The earliest questions are neutral and casual, building rapport and trust between the interviewer and the interviewee. With trust established, there is an implied permission for the interviewer to get more personal and more direct.

5. Interviewers signal their intent with transitional phrases. When the topic is going to change, they say so. They do this to provide a road map for the interviewee so there are no defensive responses because the interviewee feels ambushed. They also do this to make the conversation more natural and to provide smooth segues between topics.

6. Professional interviewers do their research before the interview. They don't conduct aimless or disjointed fishing expeditions. There are certain subjects they plan to cover, so they employ questions to steer the conversation where they'd like it to go.

7. Although they are thoroughly prepared, skilled interviewers aren't bound by a pre-determined list of questions. They don't use the same questions in every interview. Instead, they hold genuine

conversations with the people they're interviewing. They pick up on subtext and clues, following up to gather more information about what's interesting or incomplete in the responses given.

As you're listening to interviews, tally the total number of open-ended questions and the number of closed-ended questions you hear. Notice the amount of information given in response to a close-ended question as opposed to an open-ended question. Notice, too, how much more breadth and depth of information an open-ended question typically yields.

If you come across a non-celebrity interview where nearly all the questions are closed-ended, notice how guarded the interviewee seems to be. A series of closed-ended questions will sound like an interrogation. It will feel that way, too, to the interviewee. Watch for signs of discomfort when this occurs.

By contrast, watch how natural and comfortable an interviewee will be when the conversation flows smoothly and the interviewer demonstrates sincere interest in what's being said. Watch for the way people respond to questions asked. Note which types of questions cause them to relax and ease into expansive replies, which types of questions cause them to pause and reflect before they answer, and which types of questions take them by surprise. By observing the cause and effect behind how questions are asked and which types of questions are asked, you'll become more adept at crafting questions that yield precisely what you need to know to advance the sale.

Step 2: Rephrase Weak Questions

Once you've spent time listening to interviews and developing an appreciation and understanding for how much difference a quality question can make in a conversation, you'll be ready to work on this next step.

If you've jumped straight into this step without listening to interviews and observing for the differences listed in Step 1, you may find step 2 to be a bit more challenging. If you get stumped, take some time to go back and work through Step 1.

On paper, the easiest aspect of rephrasing questions is in turning closed-ended questions into open-ended ones. When we can visually see those pesky little helper verbs at the beginning of our sentences, it's easy to recognize and replace them with command statements or question words.

Unfortunately, it's not as easy to hear ourselves using these words in live conversations nor to course correct in the midst of a conversation. It takes practice to recognize your own use of closed-ended questions and more practice to retrain your brain in crafting open-ended questions. This skills practice is for increasing awareness and confidence in improving question construction.

For each of the closed-ended questions that follows, change the construction of the question without significantly changing the meaning. The object of the rephrasing is to strengthen each question so it will invite more complete responses. Here are two examples to get you started:

Closed-Ended Question: Can you tell me more about the specs?
rephrased as
Open-Ended Question: Tell me more, please, about the specs.

Closed-Ended Question: Will this be your first home purchase?
rephrased as
Open-Ended Question: What is your history as a homeowner?

Now it's your turn. For each question, eliminate any phrasing that could cause respondents to reply with a "yes" or a "no." Remember, even though others add on a few more words after the "yes" or "no" reply, you're still getting less than you would with a more

open question. To review this in greater depth, turn back to chapter 8.

Closed-Ended Question: Is this your sole location?

rephrased as

Open-Ended Question: _____

Closed-Ended Question: Are you comfortable with weekly check ins?

rephrased as

Open-Ended Question: _____

Closed-Ended Question: Have you considered a recycling plan?

rephrased as

Open-Ended Question: _____

Closed-Ended Question: Will reduced profit lead to more cutbacks?

rephrased as

Open-Ended Question: _____

Closed-Ended Question: Do you have a specific goal in mind?

rephrased as

Open-Ended Question: _____

Closed-Ended Question: Is this feature important to you?

rephrased as

Open-Ended Question: _____

Closed-Ended Question: Can you explain the differences in service?

rephrased as

Open-Ended Question: _____

Closed-Ended Question: May I ask about your decision criteria?

rephrased as

Open-Ended Question: _____

For advanced practice, ask for a little help from co-workers, friends or family members. Tell people you are working to develop better awareness about the way you phrase your questions. Explain the difference between open-ended and closed-ended questions. Ask others to say nothing more than "yes" or "no" when they hear you pose a closed-ended question. This will serve as a stark reminder to you about the limitations these questions place on conversation. Along the way, you'll have a few good laughs at yourself, too.

Most people are quite surprised when they discover just how frequently they use a closed-ended word choice when asking questions. Some feel this phrasing of questions is more polite or more accepted. It's not. Just go back to Step 1 and observe how people respond so much more completely and gratefully to open-ended questions giving them the opportunity to be heard and understood.

Rephrasing weak questions requires work in another area, too. The very weakest questions asked in needs assessment meetings are the ones that sound manipulative or like gotcha! questions. Buyers who expect sellers to take time understanding their needs respond negatively to these feeble attempts to paint the buyer into a corner. For each of the questions listed below, rephrase the question so it elicits useful information that can be used later to more elegantly advance the sale.

Wouldn't you agree this is a fantastic opportunity for you?

If I could show you how to eliminate duplication, would we have a deal?

How would you like to save 20% and get started right away?

You don't want to miss out and give your competitor this advantage, do you?

I have a lot riding on this. You're not gonna let me down now, are you?

Step 3: Identify Question Types

As a burgeoning question detective, you've been working so far in this chapter on examining the construction of questions and analyzing how they are received. You've practiced with alternative phrasing and are thinking about the ways questions can be improved so they will yield more and better information.

Remember, the best guidepost for phrasing questions effectively is your underlying intention. Your aim is to understand the needs of your buyers so you can provide superior solutions. Of course you want to close sales and book business. That's a given. This is

> This is how you can close more sales more effectively.

how you can close more sales more effectively. You will sell more and develop longer term, more loyal customers when you sell solutions to problems instead of merely pushing products.

That's why we've emphasized needs assessment questions so strongly. It's why the gotcha! questions in the previous exercise are being called out as risky. There may be a proper time and place for questions like those, but most sellers haven't developed the sophistication to use these sparingly. That's why you are being pressed here to think instead of questions that reveal buyer needs.

When guided by your intent to understand customer needs, you will also remain open and curious. You won't feel compelled to race ahead. You won't botch the close because it is ill-timed. Prematurely proposing or closing backfires because it puts the seller way out of alignment with the buyer's process. You will get to the close, and you will get there more elegantly when you slow down just enough to let your buyer keep up with you.

Along the way, guided by your intent to fully understand buyer needs and allowing your own natural curiosity to spur follow-up questions, you'll be even more effective with DISCOVER Questions®. Being able to correctly categorize the eight types of questions is what will enable you to recognize which ones you are and are not using in your needs assessment interviews.

Review chapters 12-20 about question purposes as you complete the next exercise. Each question is a clear example of a Data, Issue, Solution, Consequence, Outcome, Value, Example or Rationale Question. Your time spent in correctly identifying which is which will help you to do the same as you listen to your own and others' questions in live conversations.

Once you've completed the exercise, note the correct answers on the bottom of the facing page. You may not score 100% and that's perfectly okay. Now you know which question types to go back and review.

Identify each of these questions as one of the eight DISCOVER Questions® types. Recaps of question types appear on the facing page.

_____   What is your top priority over the next six months?

_____   What will the impact be if your current supplier runs short again?

_____   How many employees are you currently providing coverage for?

_____   Describe the before-and-after differences for me.

_____   What alternatives are you considering in contingency planning?

_____   How many students were enrolled in your program last year?

_____   Tell me more about your goal to gain 10% market share.

_____   What could we have done differently to prevent the situation?

_____   Help me understand what I can do to improve my service to you.

_____   What are your long-term plans for the business?

_____   Walk me through the steps you took to get to this decision.

_____   How important to you are perks that come with preferred status?

_____   What risks are involved if you go that direction?

_____   Describe what happened when you ran each of those promotions.

_____   What do you think about packaging with recycled materials?

_____   When will a final determination be made and by whom?

_____   What improvements do you anticipate in the coming year?

_____   Why does this particular line item matter so much to you?

_____   What can we do to make this right for you?

_____   What challenges are you preparing for in the next phase?

A Recap of DISCOVER Questions®

D	**DATA**	Gather background information, facts, proven information. Which location was the first to be opened to the public?
I	**ISSUE**	Understand customer complaint or conduct proactive service check. Please tell me more about the quality issues in our last delivery.
S	**SOLUTION**	Plant seeds for new ideas, gauge reaction to alternatives. What are your thoughts about trying a phased approach?
C	**CONSEQUENCE**	Surface risk of inaction, call attention to potential problems. What if rates go up before you proceed with refinancing?
O	**OUTCOME**	Tap into hopes, dreams & vision, learn specific plans and goals. What are your plans for cost reductions in the next budget cycle?
V	**VALUE**	Clarify priorities, learn what is most urgent, create hierarchy. What matters most to you as we implement these changes?
E	**EXAMPLE**	Draw contrast, show concerete situation, break down pros/cons. What are the primary differences in the two services you've tried?
R	**RATIONALE**	Find out why and how decision was made or will be made. Describe the process you use to evalue and select your suppliers.

Illustration 8

V – C – D – E – S – D – O – I – I – O – R – V – C – E – S – R – O – V – I – C

Step 4: Create a Question Strategy

Now it's time to put this practice into action with your own sales activities. To do so, prepare to be conscientious about everything you do in needs assessment and in asking questions with your buyers.

If you haven't routinely been asking questions, you may wonder how to get started without causing your long-term customers to be taken aback by sudden change. Many sellers express this

> **Avoid the natural urge to pounce on the first need you hear.**

concern when first beginning to use DISCOVER Questions® and the principles you've been reading about here. The short answer is "Don't worry!" Buyers, even those who are accustomed to a lack of questions, respond very favorably to DISCOVER Questions®.

You can ease into your new way of doing business by asking just a few questions at first. Soon, you'll find it's not nearly as awkward as you feared it would be. You may be pleasantly surprised by just how talkative your buyers are when the topic is one that interests them. (And you can be certain talking about themselves will be very interesting to them!)

To make yourself more comfortable asking questions, you can also explain to your customer what you are planning to do. You can describe your intent to learn more about their needs and seek permission, if you'd like, to ask questions before you begin.

If you share your intent, just be sure you stay true to it. Avoid the natural urge to pounce on the first need you hear. Take time to probe the need and to find out what additional needs there may be.

This consciousness, a heightened awareness of what you are doing, will give you the confidence and the competence you need to succeed. Your objective is to fully understand the buyer need(s) for which you can provide partial solutions or support in meeting. You'll know the time is right to advance the sale toward a proposal when you fully understand the need(s) and what it will take to provide a solution.

Keep reminding yourself this is about the broader needs of your buyers, not about the narrower needs for your product. Before the meeting, be sure you are able to make this distinction. Prepare a few starter questions to keep yourself at the top of the funnel early in your interview.

As you prepare those questions, consider your strategy for keeping the conversation natural. You won't be able to "stay in the moment" if you are bound by a long list of carefully crafted questions. Instead, select just two or three questions to open the conversation. Then be prepared to use your question construction skills on the fly. Ask follow-up questions when your curiosity has been sparked. Be sure your questions are strategically worded and of the right type to yield what you are seeking.

Here are some questions you can ask yourself as you prepare for a needs assessment meeting. Get in the habit of thinking this way about your questioning process, and you'll begin doing this automatically in time.

- What matters most to this individual? Why?

- What matters most to this business at this time?

- What may have changed recently with this buyer?

- What else do I need to know about the buyer's needs in order to create a compelling solution?

- How will I get started with a few quality questions?

The reason these questions are different from the ones you mentally weigh before your current sales calls is this: you will be entering into your future needs assessment calls with an entirely different mindset. When you start with an intent to learn about buyer needs, that intent changes the conversation you have and the results you get.

Your question strategy will keep you on course. It's a planning step to prevent you from reverting to product pitching without the firm foundation of buyer needs to build upon.

The first ten times you employ DISCOVER Questions® and the related approaches described in this book, force yourself to spend five minutes in planning mode. You can even do this on the way to the buyer meeting. Put the strategy at the forefront of your planning – this is all about advancing the sale by fully understanding the buyer's needs.

Next, plan the tactics you will use. Get specific in crafting your starter questions. Review what you already know and what more you need to know. Prepare an opening that communicates your intent. Review the eight types of questions and the discrete purposes of each type so you can efficiently and effectively gather all the information you need to advance the sale.

Step 5: Conduct Post-Mortems of Sales Calls

This is a step many sellers think they are too busy to complete. But "learning after doing" and reflection work is a hallmark of learning agility. Being able to cross-apply what you've learned in a wide variety of situations saves time, reduces mistakes and sets you apart from other sellers. To do this, you'll need to conduct autopsies of your sales calls soon after they are completed.

Like the preparation for your first sales calls using these techniques, the post-mortem doesn't need to take a great deal of time. Ideally, it would happen immediately after a sales call. Jotting down notes about each call throughout the day will give you an opportunity to compare and contrast a variety of scenarios and to see your patterns of behavior.

At a minimum, you'll want to evaluate what went well, what didn't go well, and what the impacts of your actions were. When it comes to the post-mortem on your calls with these questioning techniques, you'll also be evaluating the impact of different question types.

When sellers take notes during a sales call, this process is much easier. Capturing the question you asked and the answer given in reply enables you to track exactly which questions yielded the information you needed. You'll also be able to see which questions were ineffective in evoking useful information. And you'll immediately see the detrimental effects on conversation when you ask closed-ended or manipulative questions.

In case you're wondering how your buyer will feel about you taking notes instead of maintaining eye contact, let me assure you most buyers do not mind at all. Some feel better about sellers who take notes because they believe it demonstrates how seriously you take what they are telling you. The added benefit (for you and for buyers) is you will be more accurate and more compelling when you echo their own words back to them in proposals responding to the needs you've uncovered.

With or without notes, don't miss the opportunity to contemplate what happened in each sales call. A quick mental replay will keep you from repeating the same mistakes and will give you valuable insights for continually improving with these new skills.

If your sales manager makes four-legged sales calls with you, include him or her in your post-mortem analysis. You'll get a different point of view and observations on what you may otherwise miss. Think of yourself as a professional athlete, watching the replay so you can do better in each game. Like a professional athlete, you already know the outcome of the game. Others have already given you their opinions about what you could have done differently. You've moved on, maybe a little too hastily. In order to continually improve your game, you will have to watch those tapes.

Practice Makes Perfect

With these five skill-building steps, your work as a question detective has given you perspectives about quality questions from every angle. You've observed others asking questions, retooled questions to make them more purposeful so they yield the information you need, categorized and sorted DISCOVER Questions® into the eight purposes for asking questions, created your own strategy for integrating quality questions into your needs assessments, and analyzed your own sales calls to identify what you can work on to continue improving in your questioning skills.

Chances are you're already seeing the payoff for doing this work. For most people, the transformation in the quality of their personal conversations is noticeable almost immediately. As you become more proficient with asking quality questions, you can also expect to realize these professional benefits:

- You will differentiate yourself from other sellers. Most simply don't take the time to learn about and ask quality questions. Because you have, you will become the one seller buyers WANT to talk to. You'll get more appointments, more access, more referrals, more repeat business and more connections.

- You will enjoy higher levels of customer loyalty than sellers who merely pitch products. Because you are attuned to your buyers' processes and build trust by asking questions to create value, your buyers won't consider doing business with anyone else.

- You will advance your sales more quickly. There will be fewer stall outs, continuances and dropouts. Your buyers will be eager to meet with you again to hear your proposals and ideas. Your rate of closing will be higher, too, as you deliver solutions that are spot on in meeting the stated needs and priority values of your buyers.

- You will become more efficient in needs assessment, gathering more information with fewer questions. Your well-constructed questions with strategic purpose behind each one will yield precisely the information you're seeking. You will be steering the conversation with quality questions.

- You will feel good about the work you are doing. The noble profession of selling is served best by people like you who invest time to learn the skills of quality questioning and active listening so they can truly meet the needs of their buyers.

CHAPTER 22
Crafting Your Own DISCOVER Questions®

As you practice writing your own DISCOVER Questions® in this set of skills practice exercises, you'll progress in this manner. First, you'll write all eight types of questions using prompts to remind you of the purpose for each question. Next, you'll write questions to fit the buyers you work with and your own selling situations. Then you'll practice with the proper sequencing of questions, beginning with broader questions to probe business needs and then narrower questions to pinpoint the buyer's need for the product you're selling. Finally, you'll prepare for an actual needs assessment.

Writing questions of all eight types is easier than you think. In fact, without knowing it, you've already written all eight types of questions if you have been working through these skills practices in order. Take a look back at page 194. You rewrote eight closed-ended questions. They happen to be in order, all eight types of DISCOVER Questions®.

What makes the use of eight different types of questions very easy is understanding and appreciating the distinct purposes of all eight types. Refer back to the recap on page 199 or review Section II of this book if you are still unclear about the purpose for any of the eight types of questions.

At this juncture, what's important to know is there are eight different purposes for questions. It's also vital to understand how asking fewer types of questions limits the scope of information you'll have to work with. It's this awareness that will remind you to pause and consider deploying additional types of questions when the need arises.

This level of awareness is your aim for now. As you work through the skills practices in this chapter, your understanding and ability to quickly access all eight types will develop.

For sellers who don't develop this awareness, understanding and versatility with questions, needs assessment interviews will always lack depth. Those sellers have a vague sense something is missing and feel there is more to know just beyond their reach. Using all eight types of questions and constructing them to yield complete responses will eliminate unfinished business in needs assessment.

To advance more sales, you simply need to use more types of questions.

Question Writing Skills Practice #1

For each type of DISCOVER Question®, you'll be given a set of prompts like you'd hear in a role play exercise. Use these to write the type of question featured on that page. Although you may not work with accounts where these exact questions will be applicable, this practice exercise will make it much easier for you to write your own questions, sans prompts, in the exercises that follow.

Before you get started, here are a few additional reminders. You want your questions to be as effective as possible so be sure to keep these form, construction and intent tips in mind:

- All questions in this exercise should be open-ended and invite broad responses. Write questions that would be appropriate during the needs assessment phase of the sales process. Avoid using helper verbs at the beginning of your questions because they result in closed-ended question construction. Instead, use the seven question words and the command statement format described in chapter 8.

- Your intent with these questions is to fully understand the business needs of a unique and individual buyer. Asking quality questions replaces assumptions and sets you up for success because the buyer will articulate his or her needs. After acknowledging these needs, the buyer will be eager to find a solution to address these stated needs. The more you learn about the needs you can help resolve, the more likely you are to advance the sale to a close.

■ Defer questions about the narrower need for your product until later in the needs assessment. Start with broader questions focused on the needs of the business or buyer. You'll attach to these central needs to make your solution more compelling. Later in the interview you can ask about the needs related specifically to your product.

■ Don't ask gotcha! questions and don't pounce on the first glimmer of a need you hear. Instead, ask follow-up questions and probe all the angles of the need(s) you want to understand.

■ Steer the conversation by asking about the needs you can help resolve. Don't waste time on needs you have no way to address. Be efficient in where you take the conversation without being abrupt or uncaring as you steer clear of those areas you are unable to impact.

Data Questions

The purpose of asking Data Questions is to gather background information and to learn factual and proven details about the buyer. Data Questions ask about the past or present since the future is subject to change and, therefore, is not provable. Opinions and subjective points of view are not elicited by Data Questions.

An example of a Data Question is: "What percent of your total assets are currently in your 401(k)?" For more information on Data Questions, refer back to Chapter 13.

Here is a hypothetical situation where Data Questions would be helpful in getting the background information you need. Think of this as if it were a role play. Your objective is to craft open-ended Data Questions to draw out the information you need.

Role Play: You are a financial planner and sell direct to consumers. You need factual baseline information in order to make an appropriate recommendation for a couple planning for their retirement. **For each item listed, craft a Data Question to yield the facts you need.**

Number of children:

Current savings in college funds for those children:

Details about pension plan provided by employer(s):

Financial obligations (monthly) including mortgage and credit payments:

Total monthly income:

Issue Questions

The purpose of asking Issue Questions is to remedy or prevent any dissatisfaction the buyer may have with the seller, the seller's product or the seller's company. These can be used reactively, in response to a buyer complaint. They can also be used proactively to check on buyer preferences in a buyer/seller relationship.

An example of a reactive Issue Question is: "I'd like to resolve this so it won't stand between us, so please describe what happened when you spoke with people in our customer service and technical support departments." An example of a proactive Issue Question is: "How can I improve the quality or frequency of my communication with you?" For more information on Issue Questions, refer back to Chapter 14.

Here are two hypothetical situations where Issue Questions would be helpful in prompting the buyer to share what you need to know. For each role play, craft an open-ended Issue Question to draw out this information.

Role Play: You sell medical devices directly to hospitals. One of your largest customers, a regional healthcare system, is dissatisfied with the quality of a new product you sold them in bulk quantity for use in all their hospitals. Your main contact has received a lot of heat for this purchase and has called you to complain. Your objectives are to fully understand the issue and to give your buyer a chance to unload about this and feel heard by you. **Craft an Issue Question to help you meet these objectives.**

Role Play: You sell corporate telecommunications plans and handle private sector and government accounts. Your competitors are aggressive, and you need to be solidly positioned with your key accounts as contract renewals are approaching. **Craft a proactive Issue Question to check on an account's level of satisfaction with the sales and service you provide.**

Solution Questions

The purpose of asking Solution Questions is to generate discussion about new ideas. Solution Questions are used to draw out new ideas and alternative approaches from the buyer. They can also be used to check the buyer's initial reactions to ideas the seller may wish to offer in a later proposal.

An example of a Solution Question to stimulate new ideas from the buyer is: "What are some different ways your competitors have tackled this problem?" An example of a Solution Question to gauge buyer reaction is: "How do you feel about converting to solar power in the new locations?" For more information on Solution Questions, refer back to Chapter 15.

Here is a hypothetical situation where Solution Questions would be helpful in planting seeds about new ideas. For this role play, imagine yourself as an Executive Recruiter. You sell Executives on the idea of leaving their current companies so you can provide candidates for jobs you've been retained to recruit for. **Craft open-ended Solution Questions that will get each of these candidates thinking about an alternative they may not otherwise consider.**

Role Play: The CFO at a company based in New Jersey has the credentials and experience for a job with a larger company based in Florida. What Solution Question could you ask early in your meeting to stimulate thinking about new ideas for a career change like this?

Role Play: Your client is a Fortune 500 adding a Chief Learning Officer position. The client needs highly experienced candidates with experience in technology companies. As you make your initial inquiries, what Solution Question could you ask to gauge the initial interest of a candidate?

Role Play: Due to corporate downsizing, your client has asked you to work with three executives who will lose their current jobs. Craft a Solution Question to extract some preliminary ideas these executives may have about their next steps.

Consequence Questions

The purpose of asking Consequence Questions is to heighten your buyers' awareness of potential risks associated with their own inaction or choices. Consequence Questions also probe existing challenges.

An example of a Consequence Question is: "Although you will save money on the front end of that purchase, what are the hidden costs or unintended consequences you might encounter later?" For more information on Consequence Questions, refer back to Chapter 16.

Here are some hypothetical situations where a Consequence Question would be helpful in heightening the buyer's awareness about risks or consequences of their actions. **For each situation, craft an open-ended Consequence Question to cause the buyer to think about this.**

Role Play: You sell payroll services to mid-size companies. Your customers count on your company to handle complex tax and compliance regulations. Craft a Consequence Question for a customer who is considering making a switch to handle payroll internally.

Role Play: You sell point-of-care technology for veterinary service providers. Using your products, customers can provide on-the-spot diagnostic testing for pets. Craft a Consequence Question for a customer who is considering scaling back and using a third-party lab for diagnostic services.

Role Play: You sell promotional products (SWAG like pens, mugs and t-shirts with company logos). Craft a Consequence Question for a prospect who is considering another vendor who provides inferior quality merchandise at a lower price than your company.

Outcome Questions

The purpose of asking Outcome Questions is to get clarity about the long-term aim of the buyer. A seller who knows the buyer's hopes, dreams, plans, goals and vision is a seller who can turn product features into relevant and meaningful benefits. This seller knows how to inspire each buyer.

An example of an Outcome Question is: "Tell me more about your plans for transforming your department." For more information on Outcome Questions, refer back to Chapter 17.

Here are some hypothetical situations where an Outcome Question would be helpful in getting the information you need to inspire a buyer. **For each one, craft an open-ended Outcome Question to draw out this information.**

Role Play: You sell uniforms, accessories and safety gear to first responders. Craft an Outcome Question to learn about the risk management goals your buyers have for reducing worker's compensation and employee injuries.

Role Play: You sell document shredding services to law firms. You know every law firm needs a service like yours, but you want to differentiate yourself from the competition by understanding higher level needs. You know, too, those broader business needs might help you deliver solutions beyond the basic shredding services. Craft an Outcome Question to ask the Office Manager about the firm's long-term vision.

Role Play: You sell landscaping architecture services directly to homeowners in upscale neighborhoods. Craft an Outcome Question that will get new prospects talking about the dream designs they envision for their homes.

Value Questions

The purpose of asking Value Questions is to establish the hierarchy of priorities for the buyer, something the buyer may not have clarity about. By asking Value Questions, the seller will learn what is most important to the buyer at this time and why.

An example of a Value Question is: "Which project takes precedence for you and why is that?" For more information on Value Questions, refer back to Chapter 18.

Here is a hypothetical situation where a series of Value Question would be helpful in getting the information you need in order to pinpoint exactly what services you will offer to a buyer. Think of this as a role play and **craft open-ended Value Questions to progress through each item listed.**

Role Play: You sell transportation and logistics services and are screening a new prospect to determine what is most important in the services provided. Each of your Value Questions should probe to reveal the prioritization of features you can offer and to help you understand why each one matters.

First, you need to know which of these options will matter to the buyer – maintaining the cold chain, expediting border crossings, staffing with two drivers for faster delivery, and creating a network of hubs for distribution. Craft a Value Question to inquire about whether or not each is important.

Next, you'll need to know which of those options are the top priorities and why. Craft a Value Question to find out.

Finally, you'll want to ask a broad question to be sure there isn't something you've missed that is equally or even more important to the buyer. Craft a Value Question to explore what else might be of high priority.

Example Questions

The purpose of asking Example Questions is to help the buyer see what you are selling in a concrete way. This is done by getting the buyer to share details comparing and contrasting past experiences that are familiar to them or to give reactions to concrete examples offered. With these recollections of their own experiences or tangible examples to examine, buyers will become more comfortable making decisions and commitments that advance the sale.

An example of an Example Question is: "Take a look at these portraits I've done for other clients. I'd like to hear your reactions. Tell me what you like and don't like about each one." For more information on Example Questions, refer back to Chapter 19.

Here are some hypothetical situations where an Example Question would be helpful in moving the buyer from an abstract concept to a concrete experience. For each role play, **craft an open-ended Example Question to help the buyer visualize or experience what you have to offer.**

Role Play: You sell cloud computing solutions to multi-national companies. Your prospect is skeptical about security and doesn't really understand how cloud data storage works. Craft an Example Question that will help the buyer by making your services seem more familiar and tangible.

Role Play: You book corporate events for a luxury hotel and conference center. Your buyer has booked and coordinated events with you before. Craft an Example Question to help the buyer make mental tiebacks to past events.

Role Play: You sell direct to consumers. Your product is relatively unknown. It is a revolutionary new in-home fitness system. Craft an Example Question to help prospects visualize what it would be like to use the product and get results in muscle tone and weight loss.

Rationale Questions

The purpose of asking Rationale Questions is to understand how the buyer has made or will make decisions. Understanding the decision criteria, knowing who the decision makers and influencers will be, and getting insight on the behind-the-scenes processes impacting decisions can favorably position a seller.

An example of a Rationale Question asked before a decision is made is: "In addition to cost considerations what will be the basis for your decision?" An example of a Rationale Question asked after a decision has been made is: "Walk me through the steps you took to reach this conclusion." For more information on Rationale Questions, refer back to Chapter 20.

Here are some hypothetical situations where a Rationale Question would be helpful in getting the information you need. **For each situation, craft an open-ended Rationale Question to draw out this information.**

Role Play: You sell fiber optics to defense contractors, typically responding to RFPs. With this RFP, bidders have been invited to submit questions before making their proposal. Craft a Rationale Question that will give you clarity about the key criteria used to select a supplier.

Role Play: You sell hearing aids direct to consumers. Buyers often give up on using their hearing aids before they get accustomed to them. Craft a Rationale Question to ask a recent buyer. Your question should probe the buyer's decision to return to your business for more adjustments rather than allowing adequate time for getting used to the hearing aids.

Role Play: You are a telemarketer who relies on repeat business. A customer has just informed you she will be switching to a new supplier. Craft a Rationale Question so you can learn what led to this decision.

Question Writing Skills Practice #2

Now you're ready to write DISCOVER Questions® you can use with your own buyers. These are to be starter questions because you will need to "stay in the moment" and keep your conversations flowing naturally rather than over-relying on a set of generic questions.

This exercise provides prompts for each type of question. The prompts will serve as reminders about the discrete purpose for each one of the eight types of DISCOVER Questions®.

You may find this exercise is more productive for you if you have a particular buyer in mind when you craft your questions. Remember to keep the questions open-ended and to focus on fully understanding the broader business needs of the customer. In the next exercise, we'll shift our focus so you can also construct questions to zero in on the narrower needs a buyer may have for the product you sell.

Additionally, you will find this exercise to be more useful for you if you are deliberate in your word choice and phrasing. Review your questions for how likely they will be to truly yield the type of information you are seeking. Of course, that requires you to first make determinations about what it is you want to know. The prompts in this exercise will give you a head start in thinking this way. Use this approach when you are crafting follow-up questions, too, always considering what it is you really want to know before wasting time with ill-conceived questions.

Keep in mind that these exercises are demanding for three reasons. First, you are new to this type of question construction and to using the eight types of DISCOVER Questions®. Second, we are using the highest standards possible in these exercises so you learn to craft highly effective questions. Starting with a high standard will help you master these skills. Third, these exercises are difficult because they are artificial – when you are working in live time with real buyers, you won't have to imagine what might be said or put yourself into an unfamiliar role.

Nonetheless, these exercises are proven to help sellers like you strengthen their connections with buyers. As you become more and more proficient with DISCOVER Questions® and the complementary skills for constructing quality questions, active listening, understanding buyer needs, and advancing the sale, you will gain competence and confidence in all selling situations.

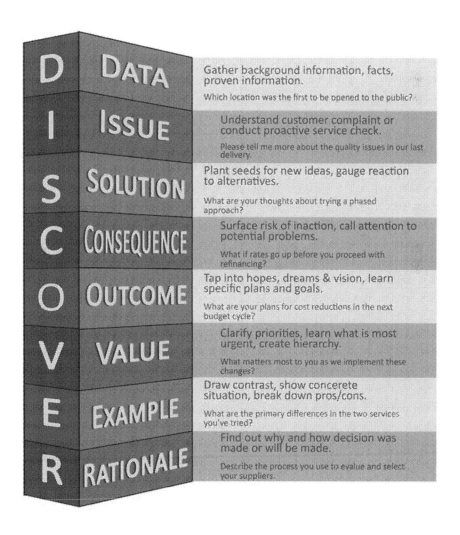

D	**DATA**	Gather background information, facts, proven information.
		Which location was the first to be opened to the public?
I	**ISSUE**	Understand customer complaint or conduct proactive service check.
		Please tell me more about the quality issues in our last delivery.
S	**SOLUTION**	Plant seeds for new ideas, gauge reaction to alternatives.
		What are your thoughts about trying a phased approach?
C	**CONSEQUENCE**	Surface risk of inaction, call attention to potential problems.
		What if rates go up before you proceed with refinancing?
O	**OUTCOME**	Tap into hopes, dreams & vision, learn specific plans and goals.
		What are your plans for cost reductions in the next budget cycle?
V	**VALUE**	Clarify priorities, learn what is most urgent, create hierarchy.
		What matters most to you as we implement these changes?
E	**EXAMPLE**	Draw contrast, show concrete situation, break down pros/cons.
		What are the primary differences in the two services you've tried?
R	**RATIONALE**	Find out why and how decision was made or will be made.
		Describe the process you use to evaluate and select your suppliers.

Data Questions

Think about a buyer you already work with or a type of buyer you frequently encounter. **Use the prompts below to write your own Data Questions** in your own voice and specific to your own buyer(s).

With Data Questions, remember not to use any language suggesting you want an opinion or a future projection. Data Questions are meant to elicit provable facts. **For each of the two categories below, write five Data Questions to get context and information**. This will influence what you offer and how you will position your solution.

Questions to learn about the history of the buyer. This might include when the business was started, family data for a B2C sale, past volumes of products like yours that have been used, etc.

1.

2.

3.

4.

5.

Questions to learn about the current state of the buyer. This might include number of locations, number of employees, sales or financial data, how current supply needs are being met, etc.

1.

2.

3.

4.

5.

Issue Questions

Think about a buyer you have worked with for a period of time and have had a complaint from in the past (or are dealing with presently). Use the prompts below to write your own Issue Questions in your own voice and specific to your own buyer.

With Issue Questions, remember the purpose is to solidify or repair the trust and relationship between you and the buyer. Issues the buyer has with other suppliers or with people inside their own organization are not probed using Issue Questions (those would most likely be probed using Consequence Questions instead). **Write at least two reactive Issue Questions and two proactive Issue Questions below.**

Questions to get a complete understanding of a situation causing buyer dissatisfaction with you, your product or your company. These are usually asked in response to a buyer complaint. Be careful not to make your questions seem defensive. Your intent is to give the buyer a chance to vent frustration and to feel they have been heard.

1.

2.

Questions to proactively understand the expectations this buyer has in order to avoid making sales or service errors that could later cause dissatisfaction.

1.

2.

Solution Questions

Think about a buyer you already work with or a type of buyer you frequently encounter. Use the prompts below to write your own Solution Questions in your own voice and specific to your own buyer(s).

With Solution Questions, remember to start with bringing out alternatives and ideas from the buyer. Later in the process of needs assessment it will be appropriate for you to offer additional ideas or alternate solutions in the form of a question to gauge the buyer's initial reactions. **Practice writing two Solution Questions for each use.**

Questions to promote buyer brainstorming and the generation of new ideas. This might include exploring alternatives the buyer used in the past, options used by competitors and peers in other markets, innovations and any other possibilities the buyer can offer as ideas.

1.

2.

Questions to check the buyer's initial reaction to your ideas. This might include asking about what's been tried in the past, feelings about something new or different and even suggestions related to minor changes.

1.

2.

Consequence Questions

Think about a buyer you already work with or a type of buyer you frequently encounter. Use the prompts below to write your own Consequence Questions in your own voice and specific to your own buyer(s).

With Consequence Questions, remember that it's not unkind to point out potential risks. It is not inappropriate to probe pain points in order to motivate your buyer to alleviate pain. It is not heavy-handed to ask questions about risks, challenges, pain points or consequences because your intent is to understand the need(s) and create a solution to help address the buyer's need(s). **Write one question for each prompt.**

Question to inquire about the current challenges or obstacles your buyer is experiencing.

Question to call attention to the negative aspects (cons) of a choice the buyer is considering.

Question to magnify the risk a buyer will be taking if they shift their business to another provider.

Question to probe the impact on others if a buyer doesn't take action.

Question to call out the possibility of unintended consequences and trickle-down effects of a buyer's choice.

Outcome Questions

Think about a buyer you already work with or a type of buyer you frequently encounter. Use the prompts below to write your own Outcome Questions in your own voice and specific to your own buyer(s).

With Outcome Questions, remember that understanding the big picture, long-term goals for the buyer will give you something inspiring to tether your proposed solution to so you can make it more compelling. Hopes, dreams, plans, goals and vision are all future-focused, so your Outcome Questions will ask about a desired or expected future state. **Write one question for each prompt.**

Question to find out what changes the buyer would like to see in the future.

Question to inquire about how these changes are being prepared for and planned.

Question to identify the goals or targets set for the buyer by senior management.

Question to understand the broader vision of the parent company and how the individual buyer's goals tie in to that vision.

Question to get a full description of the buyer's desired outcome for using your product or service.

Value Questions

Think about a buyer you already work with or a type of buyer you frequently encounter. Use the prompts below to write your own Value Questions in your own voice and specific to your own buyer(s).

With Value Questions, remember value cannot be assumed. Even if two similar buyers do, in fact, have a similar set of priorities, there will be differences to explore. The weight of importance, the reason for the prioritization and the underlying personalized benefits should all be brought to the surface. When the buyer thinks about what matters most to him or her and articulates it to a seller, the sale is practically closing itself.

Asking Value Questions gives the buyer a chance to name and claim their own priorities. This cements their own commitment to what they value. A wise seller will deliver a solution honoring what is important to the buyer. Using Value Questions also ensures you will deliver what matters most to a buyer. **Write one question for each prompt.**

Question to find out which need is the most important to the buyer.

Question to find out what makes this need the most important one.

Question to determine whether or not the products or options you might offer will be of significant value to the buyer.

Example Questions

Think about a buyer you already work with or a type of buyer you frequently encounter. Use the prompts below to write your own Example Questions in your own voice and specific to your own buyer(s).

With Example Questions, remember your aim is to help the buyer see, feel or imagine the experience (or something similar) so they will have a more concrete idea of what it will be like to own or use the product you are selling. With Example Questions, you are doing the equivalent of providing a test drive to potential buyers of a new car.

Craft a question for each prompt. Be sure your questions will generate comparisons, contrasts, visualizations or memories of past experiences so buyers can relate to what you're offering.

Question to inquire about past experiences, good and bad; using products similar to the ones you sell.

Question to ask for a direct contrast between two similar experiences. This might include two different attempts to do the same thing, using two different partners or vendors, two different time frames, etc.

Question to engage the buyer in making choices based on concrete examples shown or demonstrated. Be sure to keep this focused on making comparisons and contrasts. Questions that focus on preferences alone are more likely to be Value Questions.

Rationale Questions

Think about a buyer you already work with or a type of buyer you frequently encounter. Use the prompts below to write your own Rationale Questions in your own voice and specific to your own buyer(s).

With Rationale Questions, remember to avoid the use of the word "why." It's a trigger word and can put people on the defensive. With a Rationale Question, asking "why" could accidentally sound like you are questioning the buyer's judgment rather than seeking to understand their process for making decisions. Command statements will help you rephrase questions that would otherwise begin with the word "why."

Craft three questions for each prompt below so you will have a strong repertoire of Rationale Questions.

Questions to understand how a decision will be made. This might include who will be involved in making the decision, the criteria used to make a decision, other factors influencing the decision, the timeline for making a decision and so on.

1.

2.

3.

Questions to understand the process for how a decision was made. This is to help you know what to do differently the next time a decision is made so you can intersect sooner or more effectively in the process.

1.

2.

3.

Question Writing Skills Practice #3

This list of DISCOVER Questions® is jumbled. If asked in the proper sequence, this would be a solid needs assessment interview. Your task in this skills practice is to arrange the questions so the interview begins by asking about the broader needs of the business and ends with questions about the narrower needs for the products offered by the seller.

These are questions asked by a produce supplier working with a retail grocery buyer. Number the questions in an order that would match the question funnel described at the end of Chapter 9.

_____ What should I know to ensure your satisfaction as our customer?

_____ What quantity of the one-pound pack do you need for each region?

_____ How many stores are there in the chain?

_____ Help me understand what happens when you run a buy-one-get-one-free promotion and how that's different from no promotion.

_____ Tell me about the produce department sales goals for this quarter.

_____ How will you determine which supplier to use?

_____ How would you feel about taking two-pounders instead?

_____ What happens if you can't get the supply you need and that causes you to miss the sales goal?

_____ In your role as Director of Produce, what is most important to you?

_____ What is corporate's vision for the business?

For bonus points, identify which type of DISCOVER Question® each of these is. (Hint: there's at least one of each type.)

When you review the questions in an appropriate sequence, you can see how the seller learns about the broad business needs first. Very broad questions about the number of stores in the chain, the corporate vision, produce department goals, the impact of promotions and what is valued by the buyer belong at the top of the funnel.

Of course, these broad questions would likely have a few follow-up companions since this is to be a natural, smoothly progressing conversation. When the situation and needs are fully apparent and well-understood by the seller, it would then be time to shift to more narrowly focused questions. The narrowing of the focus would be to understand the need this buyer has for the products the seller can offer.

Narrower questions include the ones about quantity and pack size. These very specific questions are only useful once the buyer's desire has been heightened so the buyer is poised to take action.

When sellers start with narrow, product-focused questions, they miss out on identifying what really matters to the buyer. The best these sellers can do, then, is compete on price or other variables that do not engender buyer loyalty or trust. It is a weak position for a seller to adopt. It's what commoditizes your products.

Turn back to the DISCOVER Questions® you wrote in Question Writing Skills Practice #2. The exercise was set up so you were primarily crafting broad questions that would reveal broader business needs.

Your next step is to prepare the questions that would come later in the needs assessment interview. For each type of DISCOVER Question®, still thinking about the buyer(s) you wrote those broader questions for, craft a narrower question to probe the buyer's need for the product you sell.

An example of a narrow, product-focused question would be "How often do you replace the toner in each of your copiers?" This is not about the higher level needs of the business. It is about the need for toner, a product.

To develop an even keener awareness about how you sequence questions, label the questions you ask in customer interactions so you can distinguish between the ones aimed at learning about broader business needs and the ones aimed at understanding the need for your products. This simple reflection and exercise will prevent you from improperly sequencing questions. It will also remind you to include the broader questions about business needs so you won't skip straight to the product-focused questions that may be off-putting to buyers at the beginning of your meeting.

Question Writing Skills Practice #4

These 12 steps will help you develop a discipline for the skills and techniques covered throughout this book. Completing these steps will help you be more successful in connecting with buyers and, ultimately, in making more sales as a result of those connections. Some of these steps are preparation for writing DISCOVER Questions® while others involve the writing of questions. It all goes hand-in-hand.

This is the closest you should get to scripting questions for a sales call. While it is helpful to plan ahead and to prepare a few starter questions, you won't want to get tied down to a list of questions. Don't let anything prevent you from following the natural course of conversation. Outside of this skills practice, if you do prepare DISCOVER Questions® before a needs assessment interview, be sure to use them only when the conversation lags or stalls. Work on letting curiosity and your intent to fully understand buyer needs be your guide instead of a set of predetermined questions.

For the purpose of putting together all you've learned, this is an exercise to help you visualize what advancing the sale might look like using DISCOVER Questions® and the other techniques in this book. Follow the steps outlined here as if you were actually preparing for a sales call with one of your buyers. Write down your responses to each question. This will give you a handy reference for mentally preparing for later sales calls, too. It will help

> It's easier to understand the needs of your buyers when you understand your buyers.

you see what work you can be doing to improve your connections with buyers.

Each step includes the chapter number you can turn to if you need a refresher on what to do or why it matters.

Step 1: Put yourself in your buyer's shoes. See the Introduction.

It's easier to understand the needs of your buyers when you understand your buyers. The more you can see things from the buyer's perspective, the more effective you will be in anticipating, understanding and meeting the needs of that buyer.

How do you put yourself into your buyer's shoes? Initially, you will want to ask DISCOVER Questions® to learn about the buyer. Don't stop there.

> Develop business acumen so you can understand the challenges your buyers face.

Develop business acumen so you can understand the challenges your buyers face. If your customer base is one particular industry, get to know the lingo, major players, laws, norms and practices of that industry. Read trade publications. Network. Attend the trade shows, classes and conferences your customers attend. While there, invest some time in learning and growing alongside your buyers.

When you make a sales presentation to your buyer, it will be a compelling point of differentiation if you can empathize with his or her challenges and recognize pending opportunities and potential risks.

To get started, list five specific actions you can take to improve your ability to see things from your buyer's perspective.

1.

2.

3.

4.

5.

Step 2: Evaluate yourself the way a buyer would. See Chapter 1.

In this step, you'll need to be candid with yourself. Most sellers have picked up certain habits and shortcuts, impairing their effectiveness and compromising their personal brand.

Take a look back at the 12 Dimensions of Trust and use this as a tool for self-assessment. After all, this is how your buyers are assessing you so you might as well take a closer look. Trust has become the new glue for buyer/seller relationships. You can't form lasting connections without establishing and building trust. **What potential barriers to trust or breaches of trust would possibly prevent a buyer from working with you? What are going to do about this?**

Step 3: With this particular buyer, at this point in time, what is it that he or she personally values? See Chapters 2 and 4.

If you do not know enough about the buyer to answer this question, you can use Value Questions to fill in the gaps. Then you'll use what you learn to customize your presentation and to differentiate yourself from other sellers who miss sales opportunities because their generic product pitches fail to engage buyers.

Avoid proposing solutions or pitching products before you know what is of value to an individual buyer. Doing so forces you to sell from a weakened position, and there is no need to do that. It's simple to learn what matters to a buyer. Just ask!

If you think you know what a buyer values, proceed with caution. Stale information and inaccurate assumptions may lead you astray. Many a seller has made the mistake of proposing a solution without fully understanding the current priorities of the buyer. Sellers are then dazed and confused when the buyer rejects the proposal because what mattered most had changed and was not adequately addressed in the proposal.

When you are certain you can answer this question you will be ready to proceed with your proposal. The all-important question is: **With this particular buyer, at this point in time, what does he or she personally value most of all?**

Step 4: Where is this buyer in the buying process? See Chapter 3.

Once you know what the buyer needs and values, you will be ready to deliver a proposal. There may be one more reason to tap the brakes. You've got to be sure the buyer is progressing through the buyer's process to a point where the proposal will be welcomed.

233

If the buyer has not advanced to desire or action, you can use DISCOVER Questions® to build interest and desire before you proceed with a premature proposal or close. If you're not clear on how to tell where the buyer is in their own process, be sure to turn back to Chapter 3 and review the information there about the buyer's process and how the seller must stay in alignment.

Where is your buyer in the buying process? How do you know?

Step 5: With this buyer, how will you create value and differentiate yourself from other sellers? See Chapters 5 and 6.

Today's empowered buyers expect more from sellers. You have to offer relevant value, add value to win the sale **and** create value to build loyalty.

You can create value just by asking quality questions to make buyers think. Take a look back at the DISCOVER Questions® you crafted in Question Writing Skills Practice #2. Thinking from the buyer's perspective, **which of these would create value by making the buyer pause and think about big picture issues and decisions? Which ones would challenge a buyer to get better clarity on what they are doing? Which ones would stimulate new ideas and bigger picture considerations?**

This is the power of a well-constructed question. When you combine the eight types of questions, you can't help but create value for the fortunate buyers who will be on the receiving end of your questions.

Step 6: Prepare a script for how you will open the conversation with this buyer by describing your intent to ask questions so you can understand the buyer's needs. See Chapter 7.

Signaling your intent to better understand the buyer's needs makes you accountable for sticking to it. When you lay out the road map for the buyer, you also set the expectation you'll stay on course. That means you can't shift gears at the first glimmer of a need. Instead, use follow-up questions to probe a need and to find out about other needs, too. There will be plenty of time to propose a solution after you've thoroughly assessed needs.

With this in mind, write a script here for communicating about your intent.

Step 7: Work on your question construction. See Chapter 8.

Take another look at the DISCOVER Questions® you wrote in Question Writing Skills Practice #2. **Check each one to be sure it adheres to the guidelines established here for quality question construction.** Every question should be:

- Clearly phrased so it asks for exactly what you want to know.

- Focused on understanding the needs of the buyer. Remember, those are the broader needs of the individual or company, not the narrower needs for your product (that comes later).

235

- Open-ended.

- Steering where you want to go in the conversation, not meandering into needs you are unable to provide solutions for.

- Succinct and to the point so the buyer can understand what you are asking about.

Step 8: Let your natural curiosity be your guide, staying "in the moment" and asking follow-up questions that come naturally in the course of conversation. See Chapter 9.

Even if you prepare ahead and have a list of starter questions you will ask the buyer, don't let the list override your natural curiosity. When you hear something interesting, something suggesting a need you can help with, the natural and strategic response is to ask a follow-up question. Probe to learn more about the needs you can help with and to better understand any feelings or priorities expressed by the buyer.

If you leave significant statements hanging without comment or follow up, you will appear to be disinterested and self-centered. Since building trust is one of the objectives of needs assessment, you can't let a list of pre-planned questions compromise the conversation.

To stay "in the moment," how will you keep yourself tuned in for feelings and priorities your buyer expresses?

Step 9: Screen the questions you routinely ask to be sure they are not manipulative, leading, closed-ended or narrowly focused on the buyer's need for your product. See Chapter 10.

The fact you are a salesperson means your ultimate goal is to sell. Needs assessment is not a replacement for selling. It is a method of selling. In their haste to "get back to selling," some sellers entirely miss the point of conducting needs assessments.

> Needs assessment is not a replacement for selling. It is a method of selling.

DISCOVER Questions® are not weapons to be used to dominate or defeat buyers. They aren't magic tricks to manipulate buyers. They aren't formulaic, robotic or scripted with a false promise of leading a buyer into your sales trap. They are a method for understanding buyer needs so you can create compelling solutions and meet buyer needs.

If you are looking for "magic bullet" shortcuts, gotcha! questions or pre-scripted interview templates, then you will be disappointed by DISCOVER Questions® because they only work when you do.

If you've relied on leading or manipulative questions in the past, you may find them to be incompatible with the intent and techniques featured in this book. Hopefully, you've realized you don't need those old school approaches now that you are developing superior skills in crafting quality questions.

It takes time to break old habits and to replace them with new ones. Give yourself 30 consecutive days of conscientious focus on using what you've learned here. By then, you will be lapsing back into closed-ended questions and narrowly focused questions less frequently. You will also see the benefits of asking quality questions, and those positive results will keep you going so you can master these new techniques.

For now, go back and check the questions you've already written

one more time. Be sure they reflect your intent to fully understand customer needs. Set aside any questions that press for a close or otherwise don't fit in with the intent and/or timing of needs assessment. There may be a more appropriate time for using those questions.

Admittedly, we are taking a purist approach at this point. The purpose of doing so is twofold – to help you get clarity on the distinctions we're making so you can use and evaluate DISCOVER Questions® on their own merits and to shift your needs assessment tactics so you can better meet the changing expectations of empowered buyers.

Step 10: Eliminate distractions and prepare yourself to actively listen to the content and feelings your buyer shares in response to your questions. See Chapter 11.

Asking quality questions creates value for the buyer. But there's even greater value to be realized if the seller hears, understands and responds to the answers given when quality questions are asked.

Make a list here of five specific changes you can make in order to actively listen more often and more effectively. Use this as an action plan for improving your conversations with buyers.

1.

2.

3.

4.

5.

Step 11: Write DISCOVER Questions® to help you understand the needs of this particular buyer. See Chapters 13-20.

Prepare at least one of each of the eight types of questions. You may not need all eight or you may need several of just one type – there is no magic combination of questions and no particular order that is more effective than another. What makes these work is your ability to steer the conversation by using the mix of questions appropriate for each unique conversation and buyer.

D	**DATA**
I	**ISSUE**
S	**SOLUTION**
C	**CONSEQUENCE**
O	**OUTCOME**
V	**VALUE**
E	**EXAMPLE**
R	**RATIONALE**

Step 12: Stay current on new buyer research and trends.

Let's connect! Get in touch with and follow author Deb Calvert (@PeopleFirstPS) on social media and subscribe to her award-winning blog CONNECT2Sell at http://blog.peoplefirstps.com/connect2sell/rss.xml.

Deb's latest research is about B2B buyers and their preferences when it comes to how sellers behave. It turns out that buyers have a strong preference for 30 behaviors that are more commonly associated with leadership than with sales. The movement to Stop Selling & Start Leading® identifies these 30 behaviors.

The leadership behaviors come directly from a highly esteemed body of work known as The Leadership Challenge® by Jim Kouzes and Barry Posner. Deb is working directly with Jim and Barry on the research to understand how to apply these leadership behaviors in the sales arena. It's a fascinating study of what modern buyers expect and demand from the sellers they choose to do business with.

Another resource you won't want to miss as you continue learning about emerging trends in buying and selling is The Sales Experts Channel. Author Deb Calvert founded this channel to bring 63 of the world's leading sales speakers, authors, trainers, coaches and thought leaders together in one place. They've produced hundreds of on-demand webinars for sales managers and front line sellers, covering virtually every topic related to our profession. You can find these webinars – all free – at bit.ly/SalesXperts.

ABOUT THE AUTHOR

Deb Calvert, *"Discover Questions® Get You Connected"* author and Top 50 Sales Influencer, is President of People First Productivity Solutions, a UC Berkeley instructor (teaching the popular Sales Development Principles course), and a former Sales/Training Director of a Fortune 500 media company. She speaks and writes about the Stop Selling & Start Leading® movement and offers sales training, coaching, and consulting as well as the leadership development programs. She is certified as an executive and sales coach by the ICF and is a Certified Master of The Leadership Challenge®. Deb has worked in every sector and in

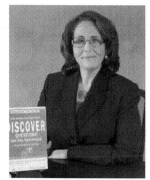

Photo by Lambert Hill Photography

14 countries to build leadership capacity, team effectiveness and sales productivity with a "people first" approach. *"DISCOVER Questions® Get You Connected"* has recently been named by HubSpot as one of the "20 Most Highly Rated Sales Books of All Time."

For more information about People First Productivity Solutions, the DISCOVER Questions® workshop or other sales training and coaching options, visit www.peoplefirstps.com or call 408-612-5918.

APPENDIX
CONNECT2Sell

This book has focused on using DISCOVER Questions® to get you connected with buyers, primarily by conducting effective needs assessment. But DISCOVER Questions® are equally effective in all sorts of sales engagements. Value Questions, for example, are extremely important in conducting effective negotiations with buyers.

While needs assessment is an important phase of a sales process for needs-based selling, it does not stand alone. At People First Productivity Solutions, we offer training in all aspects of sales, equipping sellers with the skills they need to Open, Assess, Propose, Address and Close. We teach sellers how to advance the sale from the earliest stages of prospecting through long-term account maximization following an initial close.

Here's what one highly successful seller had to say about our CONNECT2Sell training program:

> ".... I've been selling in the DC Metro area for 10 + years and everyone in my industry has known for quite some time that a major shift has occurred, but no one that I've spoken with (including top management at very large companies) has been able to identify the issue and develop a plan of attack the way that Deb has. It doesn't matter what you're selling – human behavior has changed due to the amount of data available to us on the internet and we all have to adapt accordingly and change our game plan. Deb has shown us that relationships are still important but they must be backed up with value and that value has to be emphasized and tied in every step of the way.

> This training could not have come at a better time for me. Deb has shown me how to think from the buyer's perspective and how to dig deeper to make sure that the most pressing need is uncovered. A solution that addresses that need will be high value and will trump any objection in terms of pricing or preference.

> I really appreciate the level of coaching that she provides and especially the ongoing support and feedback. She truly understands the struggles we're facing and genuinely wants to help us succeed. It has been a pleasure and I look forward to sharing many success stories with her in the near future and beyond!"

The People First Productivity Solutions training team can help your team in this same way.

We certify trainers in the use of DISCOVER Questions® and in the full CONNECT2Sell program. Certified trainers have access to a wide variety of training materials, facilitator guides, manager-led follow-up exercises to be used post-training, plus ongoing support as new research emerges and program modifications are made.

We also conduct training on site with our clients. We customize our delivery to meet the needs of your team. Our customized skills practice exercises, case studies, role plays and more make our training highly relevant for your sellers in your market and/or industry.

Our proprietary tools, including DISCOVER Questions®, are based on field research conducted with sellers in a wide variety of markets and industries. All PFPS sales trainers are professional sellers, too, giving them a high degree of credibility and an ability to make training applicable immediately.

CONNECT2Sell is available as a comprehensive training program or in modular sections. Training participants are surveyed so the needs of your team will be identified before the work of customizing the content and delivery is completed. Give us a call and we'll talk about your needs, the desired outcomes you think training may be able to help you work toward and how we may be able to assist you.

a product of People First Productivity Solutions

http://peoplefirstps.com

STOP SELLING & START LEADING
Deb's newest book with co-authors Jim Kouzes and Barry Posner!

Amy Spellman made a mid-life career change. She became an insurance agent because she wanted to help people. Amy was excited about the fresh start, income potential, and opportunity to make a difference in people's lives.

Six months later, Amy left sales. For her, the role was unfulfilling despite the higher income. Following up company-generated leads and making cold calls felt like dialing-for-dollars, and calling people multiple times felt like an imposition. Selling in a high-pressure environment meant spending less time helping people in the way she'd envisioned. Instead of feeling supportive, she felt pushy. Instead of enjoying connections with clients, she felt inauthentic, rushed, and slightly manipulative when using sales tactics she had observed and learned from others.

Perhaps you've felt the same way at some time in your sales role. Maybe you've sensed that buyers seem suspicious and guarded when you contact them. Or possibly your friends and family are cynical and question your character and integrity because you are in sales.

REDEFINING THE B2B BUYER EXPERIENCE

The pervasive, negative stereotypes about sellers affect how people initially react to you, even, on occasion, family and friends who know you well. The *Glengarry Glen Ross* and *Wolf of Wall Street* movie personas of sellers are reinforced in real life often enough to put buyers on the defensive. As Amy said, "It didn't feel like I could win. The people I called assumed I was going to take advantage of them. They didn't even give me a chance to show how I would be different." What's a seller to do?

More of the Same Behaviors Results in More of the Same Reactions

Too many sellers simply shrug their shoulders and adopt these stereotypical behaviors. Others defuse buyers' negative perceptions by operating with integrity, the more challenging path to be sure.

For buyers, the challenge is to separate the wheat from the chaff, determining which sellers are trustworthy. An overwhelming refrain from buyers in our study was, as one person said, "All sellers seem to be saying and doing the same things." Sellers, despite their intentions, are failing to behaviorally differentiate themselves.

As buyers become increasingly self-sufficient and more resistant to advances, sellers scramble to find more leads, make more calls, and get in front of more buyers. Engaging in more of the same old sales behaviors exacerbates the problem. All sellers seem the same, because they're all behaving the same way.

SOMETHING DIFFERENT, BUT WHAT?

There must be another option. Retail researchers Robin Lewis and Michael Dart concluded that winning people's wallets requires delivering "such an awesome connecting experience that they will go out of their way to come to you." "An awesome connecting experience"? Now that's something different in selling! It's a phrase that's more likely to be associated with leadership. Let's break it down.

✓ Awesome.

When we're using the slang defnition of awesome, it means the sales call is going to be "very impressive." Jaded buyers won't rate even the best selling behaviors as "very impressive." Quality is a weak differentiator that may go completely unnoticed. The dictionary meaning of awesome is more applicable: "causing an overwhelming feeling of admiration or respect." Now that's something that would certainly capture a buyer's attention and clearly be differentiating.

Anthony Iannarino, the founder of The Sales Blog, says such a response only comes with genuine caring for your buyer. He believes the power of caring is unmatched and that those who care deeply about their buyers "will stand out from the crowd and be welcomed as trusted, valued partners." Empathy, intimacy, and presence, he asserts, create the caring experience that keep buyers coming back for more.

✓ Connecting.

Connecting, too, aims for differentiation. Connecting means joining or linking. To be clear, connecting means much more than a social media link. It involves more than the initial rapport-building you do with prospects. A connection isn't just a name in your CRM. Connections aren't sufficiently made by automation and artificial intelligence (AI). In human interactions, there's a need for emotional connection.

Jeb Blount, CEO of Sales Gravy, says the point of connecting in sales is to "win other people over by making them feel that they are the center of your attention, to make them feel significant or important," and then to "nurture a deep emotional connection [because] people buy from people they like, trust, and believe will solve their problems." Buyers want authentic connections, not superficial ones that evaporate when the sale is closed

---

To read more from this new bestseller, go to <u>amzn.to/2rmWVOS</u>

Manufactured by Amazon.ca
Bolton, ON